Sifan H

A Versatile Force in Distance Running

Larry B. Berry

Table of contents

Introduction

Ethiopian-born Dutch middle- and long-distance runner Sifan Hassan is well-known for her exceptional adaptability in a variety of track competitions. Hassan was born in Ethiopia in 1993. At the age of 15, she fled her home country and took asylum in the Netherlands, where she soon started her athletic career. Her incredible endurance and speed, along with her impressive performances in events ranging from the 1,500 meters to the marathon, swiftly propelled her to fame. At the 2020 Tokyo Olympics, Hassan created history by taking home gold in the 5,000 and 10,000 meters as well as bronze in the 1,500 meters—a remarkable display of perseverance and power. Her incredible journey from refugee to world champion has captured the attention of fans worldwide, and her accomplishments have established her as one of the most renowned and adaptable runners of her generation.

The path that Sifan Hassan took to become one of the most accomplished athletes in the world is just as amazing as her accomplishments on the track. She was born in Adama, Ethiopia, but left her own country as a teenager to seek asylum in the Netherlands because of turmoil. There, juggling her studies as a nursing student, she started running sporadically. Her raw talent soon became clear, and she swiftly created a name for herself in European track contests.

Early in her career, Hassan was a dominant force in middle-distance events, especially the 1,500 meters, where she set several records and took home her first significant gold medal at the 2014 European Championships. She gradually increased her distance, becoming proficient in the 3,000, 5,000, and 10,000 meters. She also broke world records in the mile and one-hour races. She gained respect and appreciation for her bold and aggressive racing style, which frequently allowed her to hold off several rivals in close finishes.

She accomplished a historic "triple" in 2021 at the Olympics in Tokyo, taking home medals in three demanding events: bronze in the 1,500 meters, gold in the 5,000 and 10,000 meters. This achievement was even the more amazing considering the hectic schedule of the Olympics and the strategic demands of every race. Hassan has distinguished herself from her contemporaries with her ability to move between distances with ease and her mental resilience.

Hassan is a representation of tenacity in addition to her athleticism. Her inspirational story of escaping Ethiopia and rising to international fame strikes a chord with admirers everywhere. She frequently discusses using running as a means of escaping her problems and finding serenity, and many people who encounter hardship are still motivated by her narrative. In addition to being a top-tier runner, Hassan now speaks up for migrants and promotes tenacity and hope.

Her career doesn't appear to be slowing down as she keeps competing in prestigious marathons, further solidifying her reputation as a long-distance runner.

Chapter 1: who is sifan Hassan

Renowned long- and middle-distance runner Sifan Hassan represents the Netherlands in competition. At the age of 15, Hassan, who was born in Ethiopia, fled to the Netherlands. She excelled in a variety of distances, from the 1,500 meters to the marathon, and soon established herself as one of the top athletes in the sport.

Hassan became well-known throughout the world for her track exploits, especially at the 2020 Tokyo Olympics where she created history by taking home three medals: bronze in the 1,500 meters, gold in the 5,000 and 10,000 meters, and gold in both events. This amazing accomplishment demonstrated her adaptability, stamina, and mental tenacity. In addition, she is well-known for her world records in races such as the mile and the one-hour race, which demonstrate her versatility.

Beyond her sporting accomplishments, Hassan's life narrative exemplifies tenacity and perseverance as she overcame many obstacles as a refugee to become a well-known figure in sports worldwide. Many people all throughout the world, both on and off the track, find inspiration in her story.

Overview of Sifan Hassan's Career

Sifan Hassan is one of the most accomplished athletes in track and field history thanks to her career's exceptional versatility and success over a variety of distances. This is a synopsis of her career:

Early Years and Beginnings of Running

Birth and formative years: Hassan was born in Adama, Ethiopia, on January 1, 1993, and at the age of 15, he moved as a refugee to the Netherlands.

Beginning of Athletic Career: She started running competitively as soon as she moved to the Netherlands and advanced through the middle-distance running rankings quite rapidly.

Years of Breakthrough (2013–2015)

European Success: In 2013, Hassan achieved her maiden international triumph in the 1,500 meters at the European Athletics Championships, taking home the bronze medal. She won the same tournament the following year, making her the European champion.

World Stage Emergence: She demonstrated her promise on the international scene in 2015 when she earned a bronze medal in the 1,500 meters at the World Championships in Beijing.

Breaking Records and Gaining Notoriety (2016–2019)

Olympic Debut: Hassan raced in the 800 and 1,500 meters in the 2016 Rio Olympics, placing sixth in the 1,500-meter final.

Transition to Longer Distances: Hassan started concentrating on longer distances in 2018 and 2019, performing exceptionally well in the 5,000 and 10,000 meters. She ran a 4:12.33 mile to set a world record during this time, shattering the 5,000-meter European mark.

Dominance at Worlds: Showing off her incredible range, Hassan became the first athlete in history to win both the 1,500 and 10,000 meters at the same World Championships in Doha in 2019.

The historic Tokyo Olympics 2020 (to be held in 2021)

Triple-Medal feat: Hassan competed in three events at the Tokyo Olympics: 1,500 meters, 5,000 meters, and 10,000 meters, and he accomplished one of the greatest performances in track and field history. Her medals included gold in the 5,000 and 10,000 meters and bronze in the 1,500 meters. Considering the demanding schedule and unpredictable distances, this was an almost unachievable feat.

Change to Marathon from 2023 to the Present

First Marathon: Hassan switched to marathon running in 2023 and made her debut at the esteemed London Marathon. Despite having problems in the middle of the race, she finished in 2:18:33, demonstrating her perseverance and adaptability even more.

Subsequently, Hassan participated in the Chicago Marathon in 2023 and achieved a second-place finish in 2:13:44, which stands as one of the fastest female marathon speeds ever recorded.

Achievements and Records

World Records: Hassan's times in the mile (4:12.33) and the hour run (18,930 meters in 60 minutes) are world records.

Major Titles: She has won twice at the world championship (2019), many times in Europe, and twice in the Olympics.

Versatility: Hassan is well-known for her capacity to compete over a broad range of distances, including marathons and 1,500 meters, which is an uncommon accomplishment in the sport.

History and Significance

Sifan Hassan's career is evidence of both her extraordinary talent and tenacity. In addition to her ground-breaking exploits over a variety of distances, her journey from refugee to international athletic superstar has made her one of the most recognizable and inspirational individuals in contemporary track and field. Her position as one of the most accomplished runners in history is cemented by her triumph in the marathon and her ability to compete in both middle- and long-distance competitions.

Early Life and Background

On January 1, 1993, Sifan Hassan was born in Adama, Ethiopia, a city in the Oromia region. Hassan experienced the hardships of growing up in a challenging environment characterized by political instability, poverty, and conflict in Ethiopia. Though she didn't have any official training or goals in sports at the time, she frequently remembers running as a normal part of her upbringing, something she performed while playing with friends and exploring her community.

Hassan took the momentous decision to leave Ethiopia at the age of 15, leaving the country as a refugee. In 2008, she eventually applied for asylum in the Netherlands and started a new life there. After relocating to the Dutch city of Nijmegen, Hassan first concentrated on pursuing her degree and mastering the language. During her early years in the nation, she completed her nursing training and worked at a hospital.

This was the time she realized she had a knack for running. Hassan started running as a method to stay active, and her innate abilities quickly drew the attention of local coaches. She joined a local running club where she received her first official coaching and training because of her obvious raw speed, endurance, and talent.

Hassan's sports career took off in a matter of years. She started participating in local and national competitions, establishing herself as a promising middle-distance runner. Five years after coming to the Netherlands, in 2013, she was already competing internationally on behalf of her nation.

Her early experiences as a refugee and the difficulties she faced adjusting to a new nation and society influenced her character and way of thinking. Hassan frequently attributes her resilience and mental toughness, which would eventually define her athletic career, to her experiences in Ethiopia and her journey to the Netherlands.

Chapter 2: Early Career

Sifan Hassan began her early athletic career shortly after her teenage relocation to the Netherlands. Hassan first concentrated on her nursing education, but after joining a local club, she soon realized she had an aptitude for running. She began taking her training seriously three years after relocating to the Netherlands, in 2011, and she began working with instructors who were authorities in their domains. In her early races, she dominated the national stage, particularly in middle-distance events.

Revolution in the years 2013–2014

Hassan's breakthrough year came in 2013 when she gained widespread recognition across Europe. She competed in several events and quickly gained recognition for her 800 and 1,500-meter times. That year, she won the 1,500 meters at the

European Under-23 Championships and her first national medals in the Netherlands.

Her rise to notoriety was capped off by a fantastic performance in the under-23 division, where she won the bronze in the 2013 European Cross Country Championships. This result showed that she is not only a track athlete but also a versatile distance runner by showing that she can compete in cross-country running.

Hassan's career gained remarkable success in 2014. At the European Athletics Championships in Zürich, she dominated the 1,500 meters and took home her first significant gold medal. That year, she also took up the bronze in the 1,500-meter competition held at the IAAF Continental Cup. These victories solidified her place among Europe's top middle-distance runners.

Progress to the Global Scene (2015–2016): Hassan's successes in Europe swiftly extended to other regions of the world. She competed in her first World Championship in Beijing in 2015, when she placed third in the 1,500-meter competition. Her accomplishment proved she could compete with the world's best middle-distance runners and established her as one of the best in the sport.

In Rio de Janeiro in 2016, Hassan competed in the 800 and 1,500 meters at her first Olympics. Even though she placed fifth in the 1,500-meter final, she had an excellent run and learned a lot competing on the biggest sporting stage in the world. It became clear that she was a rising star with the potential for future Olympic glory even though she did not medal.

Change to Greater Lengths of Time

While still reigning supreme in the 1,500 meters, Hassan started to shift her attention to longer events by 2017—the 5,000 and 10,000 meters. She was able to adapt to these larger distances with ease thanks to her growing strength and endurance, which paved the way for even bigger successes in the years that followed.

Hassan's early career was characterized by her quick ascent, which was evidenced by her triumphs in national and international tournaments. Her resilience, work ethic, and ability to compete over a variety of distances laid the groundwork for her eventual dominance on the track. She became known as one of the world's most gifted and adaptable runners during this pivotal time.

Move to the Netherlands

Sifan Hassan's relocation to the Netherlands was a turning point in her life that affected both her path as a person and her prospects as a professional athlete. At the age of fifteen, Hassan left Ethiopia in 2008 because of the unrest and violence plaguing the area. She eventually made her home in Nijmegen after requesting asylum in the Netherlands. Hassan had to overcome several obstacles as a refugee in a foreign nation, such as adjusting to a totally new language and culture.

Hassan first concentrated on her education, going to school and training to become a nurse while working in a hospital. Running was her hobby and a method to keep active at the time; it was not her major emphasis. She was surrounded by others who saw her innate aptitude for running, including local coaches, who urged her to pursue the sport more seriously.

Hassan joined a nearby running club to start training, and she soon showed her remarkable potential. After moving to the Netherlands, she went from running recreationally to competing at the national and international levels in a matter of years. She advanced quickly in the sport thanks to her motivation and her coaches' encouragement.

She started her incredible ascent in athletics in the Netherlands, where she also made her new home. Her development into one of the best middle- and long-distance runners in the world was aided by the nation's supportive atmosphere and sporting infrastructure. Hassan's experience as a refugee and her relocation to the Netherlands both contributed to the development of her strong feeling of resilience, which would subsequently be seen in her performances on the track.

Hassan has expressed her thanks to the Netherlands for providing her with the chance to succeed both as an athlete and as a person during her career. Her transformation from refugee to internationally renowned athlete is evidence of the influence of her relocation to the nation and the prospects she encountered there.

Training and Development

Sifan Hassan's remarkable performance over a variety of distances can be attributed in large part to her training and growth as an athlete. Under the direction of numerous teachers and mentors who helped her reach her full potential, her training has changed dramatically from her early years in the

Netherlands to her world-class performances.

Initial Instruction (2011–2015)

Hassan joined a small running club in the Netherlands after seeing she had a knack for running, and it was there that she got her first coaching. Her early training was mostly centered on middle-distance running, where she excelled in the 800 and 1,500 meters. Under the direction of Dutch coaches, she worked diligently to improve her technique, endurance, and speed, which enabled her to go from being a recreational runner to a competitive athlete.

Her innate endurance along with intense training made for quick improvement. Hassan's training during these early years consisted of a combination of cross-country, interval, and track work to increase her strength and endurance.

Her training increased as she started competing internationally, getting her ready for longer races and more challenging opponents.

Coaching and Professional Development (2016–2018)

By 2016, Hassan was working with elite instructors who saw that she could go further in her training. Renowned coach Alberto Salazar, who oversaw the Nike Oregon Project when she started training, helped her hone her speed and aerobic ability. Salazar concentrated on teaching Hassan how to run faster in middle-distance races like the 1,500 meters while also building up her endurance.

Hassan received advanced training under the Oregon Project, which included VO2 max conditioning, altitude training, and extremely specialized exercise regimens designed to increase her resilience and endurance over a range of distances. She was pushed to enhance her racing strategies, pacing, and mental toughness by training with other top athletes. Hassan started to shatter records, establish personal bests, and extend her dominance from 1,500 meters to longer races, such as the 5,000 meters, during this time.

Shift to Extended-Range Events (2019–2021)

Hassan's training focused more on long-distance competitions, such as the 10,000 meters, as her career developed. She changed her training to emphasize both endurance and speed, which enabled her to compete in a variety of competitions. Her regimen frequently included lengthy runs, strength training, cross-training, high-intensity interval training (HIIT), and over 100 miles of running per week.

At the World Championships in Doha in 2019, Hassan accomplished a historic double by winning gold in both the 1,500 and 10,000 meters—a feat that called for a special combination of speed and endurance. Her accomplishments in these varied competitions demonstrated the fruit of her well-thought-out training program, which was created to improve her capacity to recover rapidly in between races and sustain top form throughout a range of distances.

Olympic Triumph and Further Ahead (2020–Present)

Hassan's training regimen was designed to get her ready for a historic challenge: racing in the 1,500, 5,000, and 10,000 meters in one Olympic Games—all before the 2020 Tokyo Olympics, which will take place in 2021. She received specialized training in recuperation, pace, and mental toughness to manage the mental and physical strain of competing at such a high level in a variety of disciplines. She spent a lot of time honing her race tactics, particularly in handling the strategic elements of championship racing.

She created history at the Tokyo Olympics by winning two gold medals (the 5,000 and 10,000 meters) and one bronze medal (1,500 meters), solidifying her reputation as one of the sport's most versatile runners. Her training paid off.

Training for a marathon (2023)

Despite experiencing cramps throughout the race, Hassan made a smooth transition to marathon racing in 2023, winning her first marathon at the London Marathon in a pace of 2:18:33. She covered a lot more ground in her training for the marathon, extended her endurance sessions, and made particular adjustments to meet the demands of the course.

Her innate endurance and focused training program helped her adjust to the lengthier race even though she was new to the sport, demonstrating her aptitude for even longer distances. To prepare for the demands of the 42.195 km race, Hassan trains for the marathon using a mix of long-distance endurance training, tempo runs, and nutrition and recovery techniques.

Crucial Elements of Her Education

Interval Training: To increase her speed and anaerobic ability, Hassan often uses interval training. She frequently works out on the track to help her maintain a quick pace in competitions.

Endurance Work: A vital component of Hassan's training is long-distance and tempo running, which help her develop the endurance required for events ranging from 1,500 meters to the marathon.

Altitude Training: Hassan uses altitude training, similar to many other elite distance runners, to increase her red blood cell count and improve her endurance.

Strength and Conditioning: To avoid injuries and preserve muscle endurance over extended distances, she also emphasizes strength training, which consists of core exercises and strength exercises.

Mental Conditioning: A major component of Hassan's training is developing her mental fortitude. She practices techniques to control her tension on race day, recuperate rapidly, and adjust to changing conditions.

Training for Sifan Hassan has been a dynamic process of ongoing adaptation, with an emphasis on her special capacity to race over a variety of distances. Her accomplishments are a result of her intense training, mental toughness, and physical conditioning.

Breakthrough in Middle-Distance Running

Early in the 2010s, Sifan Hassan made strides in the middle distance running world and became well-known both in Europe and internationally. Hassan started out racing in shorter events, such as the 800 meters, but she soon moved up to the 1,500 meters, where she showed her prowess and started to dominate.

Early Indications of Skill (2013–2014)

When Hassan started representing the Netherlands in international competitions in 2013, it was her first significant breakthrough. That year, she earned the bronze medal in the 1,500 meters at the European Athletics Under-23 Championships, indicating her debut as a developing prospect. She also participated in the European Cross-Country Championships, where she placed third in the under-23 division, showcasing her ability to succeed in both cross-country and track-running competitions.

For Hassan, 2014 was a turning point in her career as she established herself as one of Europe's best middle-distance runners. Her first significant international victory came when she won the gold medal in the 1,500 meters at the 2014 European Athletics Championships in Zürich. Her winning time of 4:04.18 demonstrated her capacity to compete under duress and seize the lead in the last miles of the race. This triumph was a turning point since it made Hassan a serious contender in the European middle-distance running scene.

Shift to the International Scene (2015)

Hassan started competing more frequently on the international scene after her victory in Europe, and 2015 proved to be a turning point in her career as an international competitor. She ran a personal best of 4:09.34 in the 1,500-meter final to win the bronze medal at the 2015 World Championships in Beijing. With this accomplishment, she established herself as one of the world's greatest middle-distance runners and gained invaluable experience taking on the best racers in her category.

She won the IAAF Diamond League title in the 1,500 meters that same year. She has been a consistent performer in the world's best track meets. Her triumph over elite opposition in the Diamond League demonstrated her ability to compete at the greatest levels and helped her obtain additional notoriety.

The Olympics and Ongoing Achievement (2016)

With her debut at the 2016 Rio Olympics, where she raced in both the 800 and 1,500 meters, Hassan's breakthrough in middle-distance running continued. She qualified for the 1,500-meter final and placed a creditable sixth, just missing out on a medal. Considering the high caliber of competition, her performance was amazing even though she did not place on the podium, and it paved the way for much greater success in the years to come.

During this time, Hassan's trademark in middle-distance races was her combination of unmatched speed, astute tactical judgment, and a superb finishing kick. She was a favorite in events like the 1,500 meters because of her ability to surge in the last lap, which frequently gave her the advantage in close races.

Change to Greater Lengths of Distance (2017–2018)

Even though Hassan was still competing in the 1,500 meters, she started experimenting with longer distances and was successful right away, like the 5,000 meters. Her training changed to concentrate on increasing endurance while preserving the pace required for middle-distance competitions. Because of her adaptability, she was able to maintain her success in the 1,500 meters while getting ready for longer events.

With a performance of 4:19.89 in the indoor mile in 2017, she broke the European mark, proving her superiority in middle-distance running. After winning bronze in the 1,500 meters at the 2018 European Championship the following year, Hassan started to participate frequently in middle- and long-distance races.

Middle-Distance Running's Legacy

While Hassan eventually shifted her attention to long-distance competitions, her success in middle-distance running established the groundwork for her extraordinary adaptability. She became one of the most formidable middle-distance runners of her generation with her dominance in the 1,500 meters and her world-class achievements in the 800 and mile races. She was a force to be reckoned with, and her tactical skill, resilience, and mental toughness prepared her for her eventual victories at the World Championships and the Olympics.

Chapter 3: Major Competitions

Throughout her career, Sifan Hassan has participated in a number of important international championships, frequently turning up remarkable performances across a variety of distances. The tournaments she won are broken down here, starting with the biggest ones.

1. Championships in Europe (2014, 2018)

2014 (Zürich): This tournament was Hassan's first significant global success. With a powerful closing kick, she won gold in the 1,500 meters, her first European title, and became one of Europe's best middle-distance runners.

Hassan participated in the 1,500 and 5,000 meters in Berlin in 2018. Her ability to excel over a variety of distances was further demonstrated when she won gold in the 5,000 meters and bronze in the 1,500 meters.

2. World Cups in 2015, 2017 and 2019

2015 (Beijing): Hassan's first significant achievement on the international front came when she won a bronze medal in the 1,500 meters. Her ranking as one of the world's best middle-distance runners was validated by her performance.

2017 (London): Although she didn't medal in this event, Hassan changed her focus to longer distances, placing fifth in the 5,000 meters and competing in the 1,500 meters.

2019 (Doha): She made history at the 2019 World Championships by becoming the first athlete to win gold in both the 1,500 and 10,000 meters at the same competition, which was one of her greatest career accomplishments. This incredible double demonstrated her adaptability, endurance, and tactical skill.

3. Olympic Games in 2020 and 2016

2016 (Rio de Janeiro): Hassan made her Olympic debut in the 800 and 1,500 meters, placing fifth in the 1,500 meters final. Though she didn't medal, the experience gained from this tournament was vital for her future success.

2020 (held in Tokyo in 2021): Hassan made history with his Olympic performance in Tokyo. Three events were held in which she participated: the 1,500, 5,000, and 10,000 meters. Her accomplishments were astounding:

Gold in the 5,000 meters: With a powerful sprint finish, Hassan commanded the final.

Gold in the 10,000 meters: With a magnificent last lap, Hassan completed a hard-fought golden double.

Bronze in the 1,500 meters: Despite a demanding schedule, Hassan showed off her remarkable mental fortitude and endurance to clinch a podium finish.

Hassan became the first athlete to win medals in all three of these events at the same Olympics, solidifying her position as one of the best distance runners in history.

4. Multiple Years in the Diamond League

Hassan has consistently performed well in the IAAF Diamond League, the top circuit for track and field events, across her career. Even though she frequently faced the greatest athletes in the world, she has won numerous competitions in the mile, 5,000 meters, and 1,500 meters.

Her victory in the 1,500 meters in the 2015 Diamond League championship cemented her status as one of the world's best middle-distance runners.

5. The 2015 European Indoor Championships

Hassan excelled indoors as well, taking home the gold medal in the 2015 European Indoor Championships in the 1,500 meters. She now has a longer record of accomplishments from European tournaments thanks to this victory.

6. 2016 and 2018 World Indoor Championships

Hassan proved she could race at a high level both indoors and outdoors when she won the silver medal in the 1,500 meters at the 2016 World Indoor Championships.

At the 2018 World Indoor Championships, she won bronze in the 3,000 meters, showing her flexibility by medaling in both middle- and long-distance indoor races.

7. The 2023 Marathons

Hassan switched to marathon running in 2023 and competed in her first race in the London Marathon. She encountered difficulty during the run, but she finished the marathon in an outstanding 2:18:33. This win opened a new chapter in her career and demonstrated that she was a talented road racer in addition to a track competitor.

She participated in the Chicago Marathon later in 2023 and placed second with a time of 2:13:44, which is among the fastest marathon times ever recorded. This remarkable accomplishment further cemented her long-distance running career.

8. International Records

In the mile, Hassan holds the record with a time of 4:12.33, set in 2019.

In 2020, she broke the world record for the fastest one-hour run, covering 18,930 meters in 60 minutes.

Sifan Hassan has demonstrated her capacity to compete at the top level in a range of sports, including marathons, long-distance races, and middle-distance track meets. Her reputation as one of the most talented and adaptable athletes in distance running history has been cemented by her triumphs in major marathons, the Olympic Games, and world championships.

European Athletics Championships

The European Athletics Championships are a significant biannual track and field competition that attracts the best athletes from Europe. Sifan Hassan has excelled in these events. Especially in her early years when she established herself as one of the best middle- and long-distance runners in Europe, these championships have been significant turning points in her career. An outline of her results at the European Athletics Championships is provided below:

Zürich, 2014: European Athletics Championships

1,500 meters were the event

Gold Medal as a result

Moment: 4:04.18

The first significant achievement for Sifan Hassan on the international scene came at the 2014 European Athletics Championships. Hassan put on an incredible show in the 1,500-meter final to take home the gold medal and gain the title of European champion. She was able to win the title thanks to her tactical skill and powerful finishing kick in the last lap. Her career took a significant turn after this win, which made her a well-known middle-distance runner in Europe.

2018 Berlin hosts the European Athletics Championships

Activities: 1,500 and 5,000 meters

Results: 5,000 meters gold medal

Bronze in the 1,500-meter event

Hassan had already made the switch to competing over longer distances by the start of the 2018 European Athletics Championships, but she was still strong in middle-distance races. Her dual participation in the 1,500 and 5,000 meters showcased her remarkable adaptability.

With a time of 14:46.12, Hassan won the gold medal in the 5,000 meters, demonstrating her superiority over the longer distance. Her ability to control the race and pull away in the last few laps was a credit to her endurance and tactical sense, as she won this race.

Hassan took home the bronze in the 1,500 meters. Even though she was one of the favorites, she had fierce competition but managed to place third and earn another medal in the middle-distance competition.

Relegation at the European Championships for Athletics

Hassan's growth as a top-tier runner has been significantly influenced by the European Championships. In addition to winning her important international titles in 2014 and 2018, her results in those years equipped her for success in upcoming international tournaments such as the World Championships and the Olympics. Her confidence and reputation as a formidable force at all distances were greatly enhanced by her victories.

Her supremacy in the international arena, where she went on to accomplish unprecedented feats in both middle-distance and long-distance events, was built on her success at the European level.

IAAF World Championships

At the IAAF World Championships, which are now called the World Athletics Championships, Sifan Hassan has had an incredible career. She has made a name for herself as one of the most accomplished and adaptable middle- and long-distance runners. Her achievements in these competitions have cemented her reputation as a top runner in the globe. An overview of her standout performances at the IAAF World Championships is provided below:

Beijing, China, 2015 World Championships

1,500 meters were the event

Bronze Medal as a result

Moment: 4:09.34

Sifan Hassan made her first major impression on the world stage at the 2015 World Championships in Beijing. She participated in the 1,500-meter competition and took home the bronze medal, her first-ever podium result at the World Championships. Hassan showed her tactical prowess and capacity to contend with the world's top middle-distance runners in the fiercely fought race. With this medal, she made history by proving she could compete internationally at the greatest level.

World Championships in 2017 (London)

The 1,500- and 5,000-meter events

Results: in the 5,000 meters, fifth place eliminated in the 1,500-meter semifinals

Hassan ran in both the 1,500 and 5,000 meters at the 2017 World Championships in London, indicating her increasing interest in longer distances. She had great endurance in the 5,000 meters, finishing in fifth place, just missing out on a medal. Considering her prior success in the event, her elimination in the semifinals of the 1,500 meters came as a surprise. Notwithstanding these results, Hassan saw the 2017 championships as a teaching opportunity as she developed into a more adaptable runner who could participate in both middle- and long-distance competitions.

Event Schedule for the 2019 World Championships in Doha: 1,500 meters and 10,000 meters

Results: Gold Medal in the 1,500 meters

The 10,000-meter gold medal

Sifan Hassan's career reached its zenith at the 2019 World Championships in Doha, where she achieved an unparalleled feat and created history. At the same World Championships, she became the first athlete in history to win gold in both the 1,500 and 10,000 meters. With a time of 30:17.62 in the 10,000 meters, Hassan captured her first gold medal of the competition. She had never run the distance before, but she ran a fantastic race, fighting off fierce opposition with a dominant finish. She dominated the last laps, demonstrating her endurance and mental toughness.

Hassan won her second gold medal in the 1,500 meters a few days later with an incredible time of 3:51.95, which is among the fastest times in history. She completely destroyed the competition thanks to her speed and tactical prowess in the last lap. Her status as one of the world's best middle-distance runners was cemented with this accomplishment.

Events at the 2023 World Championships in Budapest are 1,500, 5,000, and 10,000 meters.

Results: 1,500-meter bronze medal
Silver Award for the 5,000-meter event
fifth in the 10,000-meter race
Hassan once again showed her extraordinary versatility at the 2023 World Championships in Budapest by competing in all three long-distance events: the 1,500 meters, 5,000 meters, and 10,000 meters. She had a demanding schedule, but she did well in every aspect:

Hassan added the bronze medal to her already impressive list of middle-distance victories in the 1,500 meters.

She finished strongly in the 5,000 meters and took home the silver medal, narrowly missing out on the gold.

Hassan was fifth in the 10,000 meters, which was a fantastic result in a taxing event, especially considering her racing schedule.

Relegation at the World Cup

After her accomplishments at the IAAF World Championships, Sifan Hassan will always be remembered as one of the most skilled and adaptable distance runners in history. From her 2015 debut to her incredible double gold in 2019 and her sustained success in 2023, Hassan has consistently demonstrated her ability to compete and succeed at the greatest level over a variety of distances. Her unmatched ability to succeed in both long-distance (10 000 meters) and middle-distance (1, 500 meters) races makes her a singular personality in the world of sports.

Olympic Games Success (Tokyo 2020)

Sifan Hassan's incredible performance at the Tokyo 2020 Olympics—which were rescheduled from 2020 to 2021 due to the COVID-19 pandemic—solidified her reputation as one of the most adaptable and resilient competitors in Olympic history. Hassan competed in three demanding events: the 1,500-, 5,000-, and 10,000-meter runs. His accomplishment over these distances was an incredible display of fortitude, mental toughness, and tactical skill.

Event 1: Gold Medal, 5,000 Meters

Gold Medal as a result

Moment: 14:36.79

After a flawless performance from a tactical standpoint in the 5,000-meter final, Hassan won her maiden medal. She maintained her composure over the initial laps and positioned herself strategically within the front group. With her trademark finishing kick, Hassan surged ahead of her rivals to win gold in a time of 14:36.79 as the race entered its closing laps. Her speed, endurance, and tactical prowess were evident throughout her Olympic campaign, and this triumph set the tone for the remainder of it.

Event 2: 1,500 meters - Bronze medal outcome

Moment: 3:55.86

Hassan made it through the semifinals and heats of the 1,500 meters despite her demanding schedule. Among the world's top middle-distance runners was the very competitive field Hassan faced in the final. Hassan battled valiantly in the 1,500 meters, finishing in third place to win the bronze medal with a time of 3:55.86, despite having already won gold in the 5,000 meters. Her amazing physical and mental endurance was demonstrated by her ability to bounce back and compete at such a high level after several races.

Event 3: Gold Medal, 10,000 Meters

Gold Medal as a result

29:55.32

For the 10,000 meters, Hassan saved her most dramatic performance. Even though Hassan had already participated in two physically and psychologically taxing events, she entered the 10,000-meter final with the same unwavering dedication that had defined her whole Olympic journey. The race was a hard, tactical battle, but in the last meters, Hassan exploited her incredible pace to pull clear of the field and win her second gold medal in 29:55.32. Her triumph demonstrated her versatility since she won the lengthy and taxing

10,000 meters in addition to the shorter 5,000 meters.

Total Outcome

Hassan accomplished a rare feat at the Tokyo Olympics by winning gold medals in the 5,000 and 10,000 meters as well as a bronze in the 1,500 meters. Her amazing range, endurance, and capacity for recuperation in between races made her the only athlete, male or female, to win medals in all three disciplines at a single Olympic Games.

Tokyo 2020's Legacy

Sifan Hassan achieved one of the most amazing feats in distance running history with her performance at the 2020 Tokyo Olympics. It is a unique achievement to compete in so many different competitions and to triumph at the top level under intense competition. Her unwavering perseverance, capacity to overcome both physical and mental exhaustion, and exceptional tactical acumen have cemented her status as one of the best Olympians in history.

Her achievements at the Olympics, especially her double gold in the 5,000 and 10,000 meters, improved her standing internationally and demonstrated her versatility as one of the sport's most gifted athletes.

Chapter 4: World Records and Achievements

Throughout her remarkable career, Sifan Hassan has set several world records and accomplished a great deal, making her one of the most accomplished and adaptable middle- and long-distance runners. Her remarkable talent and versatility are demonstrated by her ability to set records over a variety of distances, from the mile to the marathon. An outline of her major world records and accomplishments is shown below:

Global Records

Mile World Record (2019)

When: 4:12.33 Where: Monaco

Date: 12 July 2019

At the Monaco Diamond League meeting in 2019, Hassan broke the previous mark of 4:12.56, set by Svetlana Masterkova of Russia in 1996, to create a new world record in the mile. With this record, she established herself as one of the greatest in the world at the time by showcasing her amazing speed and stamina over middle-distance competitions.

World Record for One Hour (2020)

Covered distance: 18,930 meters

Place: Brussels

Date: 4 September 2020

When Hassan ran 18,930 meters in 60 minutes during the Diamond League competition in Brussels, he broke the one-hour world record. This competition measures an athlete's hourly running distance, and Hassan's effort surpassed the previous record of 18,517 meters, which was achieved in 2008 by Dire Tune of Ethiopia. The record served as evidence of Hassan's remarkable endurance over extended distances.

5,000 meters (2020—the previous world record)

Location: Hengelo, Netherlands; Time: 14:22.12

Date: June 6, 2021

With a time of 14:22.12, set at Hengelo, Netherlands, Hassan temporarily held the world record for the 5,000 meters. Just two days later, though, Ethiopia's Letesenbet Gidey smashed this record. Even though Hassan's world record didn't last long, it showed that she was capable of running among the quickest times in the history of this competition.

Achievements at the Olympics and World Championships

Olympic Games Tokyo 2020 (2021)

In the 5,000 meters, gold medal

The 10,000-meter gold medal

Bronze in the 1,500-meter event

Hassan created history at the Tokyo 2020 Olympics by taking home gold in the

5,000 and 10,000 meters in addition to a bronze in the 1,500 meters. She demonstrated her amazing range and endurance and became the first athlete in history to medal in all three disciplines at a single Olympic Games. She was undoubtedly one of the best distance runners in Olympic history with her feat.

World Championships in Doha, 2019

In the 1,500 meters, the gold medal

The 10,000-meter gold medal

Hassan made history in the 2019 World Championships in Doha by becoming the first athlete to win gold in both the 1,500 and 10,000 meters at the same event. Her adaptability and supremacy across distances, from middle- to long-distance races, were highlighted by this incredible double.

Championships in Europe (2014, 2018)

2014 gold medallist in the 1,500 meters

2018 Gold Medal for the 5,000 meters

In the 1,500 meters, bronze medal (2018)

At the European Athletics Championships, Hassan has demonstrated consistency, taking home gold in both the 1,500 and 5,000 meters in 2014 and 2018. Her accomplishments on the international scene were made possible by her success in Europe.

Other Prominent Accomplishments

2023 London Marathon

Outcome: Time of Winner: 2:18:33

Given the difficulties she encountered during the race, Hassan's 2:18:33 victory in her first marathon at the 2023 London Marathon is astounding. This victory further highlighted her versatility across various distances by demonstrating her ability to switch to road racing and compete at the best level in the marathon.

Chicago Marathon scheduled for 2023

Second place was the outcome.

Moment: 2:13:44

Hassan ran the Chicago Marathon later in 2023 and placed second, recording one of the fastest female marathon performances ever with a timing of 2:13:44. Only months after her debut, this race cemented her place among the elite marathon runners.

Titles in the Diamond League

Hassan has participated in the IAAF Diamond League on a regular basis, taking home multiple victories and the 1,500-meter Diamond League title in 2015. She has further cemented her status as a formidable force in middle- and long-distance running with her consistent performances in this elite track and field series.

Sifan Hassan's accomplishments and world records demonstrate her extraordinary adaptability; she has won gold in numerous Olympic and World Championship events in addition to setting a world mark in the mile. She is now considered one of the best distance runners of all time thanks to her historic double in the 1,500 and 10,000 meters at the 2019 World Championships and her three-medal effort at the Tokyo 2020 Olympics. Hassan keeps pushing the envelope of what is conceivable in the sport of athletics, whether it be in road races or on the track.

World Record in 1 Mile (2019)

On July 12, 2019, during the Diamond League meeting in Monaco, Sifan Hassan broke the world record in the one-mile race. She broke the previous record of 4:12.56 established by Svetlana Masterkova of Russia in 1996 with her amazing time of 4:12.33. The mile is one of the hardest middle-distance races, demanding both speed and endurance, so this was an incredible accomplishment.

Important Information in the Record:

Time: 4:12.33

Event: Diamond League of Monaco

Prior Record: 4:12.56 set in 1996 by Svetlana Masterkova

Relevance of the Document:

This world record proved Hassan's supremacy in middle-distance running, marking a significant turning point in her career. The 1-mile race calls for both extraordinary physical stamina and exact pace, and Hassan's capacity to keep up such a rapid pace throughout the competition demonstrated her extraordinary competence and adaptability.

Her 1-mile performance demonstrated her versatility, as she could compete in events ranging from 1,500 meters to 10,000 meters. Her world record-setting was a turning point that prepared her for her historic victories at the 2019 World Championships and the 2020 Olympics in Tokyo.

World Record in the 1-Hour Race

At the Diamond League meeting in Brussels on September 4, 2020, Sifan Hassan set a new world record for the one-hour race. Athletes compete in this unusual endurance race by running for 60 minutes and trying to get as far as they can in that period. With a distance of 18,930 meters (11.76 miles), Hassan broke the previous world record of 18,517 meters, which was set in 2008 by Dire Tune of Ethiopia.

Important Information in the Record:

11,76 kilometers, or 18,930 meters, were covered.

The Brussels Diamond League

Date: 4 September 2020

Prior Record: Dire Tune's 18,517 meters (2008)

Relevance of the Document:

This world record demonstrated Hassan's extraordinary mental fortitude and endurance, as the one-hour race is a true test of physical endurance. Her season was severely disrupted by the COVID-19 pandemic, giving her fewer opportunities to practice and compete in optimal conditions, which made her accomplishment all the more remarkable.

Hassan's performance in the one-hour race showed her adaptability and capacity to win longer, endurance-based races in addition to middle-distance events. Her status as one of the most accomplished and versatile distance runners in contemporary athletics was further cemented by her world record.

Other Significant Wins and Records

Apart from setting world marks in the mile and 1-hour race, Sifan Hassan's many other noteworthy victories and records demonstrate her supremacy in middle- and long-distance running. Some of her most notable accomplishments are listed below:

Additional Notable Victories and Accomplishments

European Championships in Athletics

In 2014, she won the gold medal in the 1,500 meters in Zurich (4:04.18), becoming well-known in European athletics as the first major international champion.

2018 Berlin: Gold Medal in the 5,000 meters (14:46.12) - She won her second European gold medal by dominating the competition.

In the 1,500 meters, bronze medalist (4:03.81).

Titles in the Diamond League

Over her career, Hassan has won many Diamond League events, most notably the 1,500, 3,000, and 5,000 meters. Her reputation as a versatile athlete was cemented and her racing strategies were refined thanks to these victories over elite fields. One of the greatest titles in the yearly track and field competition, she took home the Diamond League title in the 1,500 meters in 2015.

2018 World Half Marathon Championships (Valencia): Bronze Medal (1:06:11) in the half marathon - This was her first significant road running accomplishment and demonstrated her ability to go from shorter track distances to longer road distances.

2023 London Marathon Winner, clocking in at 2:18:33 for her first marathon Hassan defeated a formidable field despite obstacles encountered during the race, including a side stitch, to win her inaugural marathon in London. Her ability to transition from track distances to one of the most difficult events in athletics was demonstrated by this victory.

With a time of 2:13:44, a European record and among the fastest marathon times ever recorded, she placed second in the 2023 Chicago Marathon. Even though it was only her second marathon, her effort solidified Hassan's status as one of the best in the world.

Additional Records European Record in the 10,000 Meters, held by Sifan Hassan (2021)

Location: Hengelo, Netherlands; Time: 29:06.82

Date: June 6, 2021

In Hengelo, Netherlands, Hassan ran a 10,000-meter time of 29:06.82, shattering the previous European mark. For a brief period, she was the world record holder, until Letesenbet Gidey beat her with a 29:01.03 time just two days later. Still, Hassan's European record stands as one of the fastest in history and cemented her supremacy in long-distance track competitions.

European Record for 5,000 Meters (2021)

Location: Hengelo, Netherlands; Time: 14:22.12

Date: June 6, 2021

Hassan broke the European record in the 5,000 meters with a time of 14:22.12 at the same event as she set the 10,000-meter record. Even though Letesenbet Gidey eventually broke her world record, this was still an incredible effort and among the quickest timings in the event's history.

European Half Marathon Record (2019)

Location: Copenhagen, Denmark; Time: 1:05:15

Date: 15 September 2019

At the Copenhagen Half Marathon, Hassan ran a half marathon time of 1:05:15, setting a new European record. Her ability to dominate larger distances outside of the track was further showcased by this record-breaking performance, which also showed off her skills on the highways.

Total Legacy

Throughout her career, Sifan Hassan has demonstrated adaptability throughout a variety of distances, including the 1,500 meters and the marathon. World records, numerous gold medals from the Olympics and World Championships, and noteworthy victories in track and road running competitions show off her extraordinary versatility as a top competitor over a variety of terrains and lengths.

She is regarded as one of the most dominant and versatile athletes in modern athletics because of her remarkable accomplishments in the mile, 5,000, 10,000, and road races.

Chapter 5: Versatility in Distance Running

Sifan Hassan is one of the most successful and distinctive athletes in track and field history because of her exceptional versatility in distance running, a unique talent that is seldom found in athletes. In contemporary athletics, her capacity to compete and triumph throughout a wide variety of distances—from the 1,500 meters to the marathon—is unmatched. She differs from many other elite runners, who usually focus on one or two distances, in that she is versatile.

Important Elements of Hassan's Multi-Dimensional Versatility Success

In both middle-distance (1,500 meters) and long-distance competitions (5,000 meters, 10,000 meters, half marathon, and marathon), Hassan has demonstrated exceptional performance. Her triumphs in these wildly disparate races attest to her special blend of quickness, stamina, and tactical awareness.

She has demonstrated incredible speed and tactical acumen in the 1,500 meters, as seen by her mile world record of 4:12.33. On the other hand, she demonstrates the endurance required to keep up a demanding pace for 25 laps in the 10,000 meters.

Flexibility on Various Surfaces and Situations

Hassan has demonstrated that she can switch between road races and track races with ease. The physical and tactical demands of road running are difficult for many athletes to adapt to, but Hassan has been successful in both. Her capacity to adapt is demonstrated by her half marathon triumphs and her outstanding marathon debut at the 2023 London Marathon, which she completed in 2:18:33.

She is mainly recognized as a track athlete, but she is also capable of handling the longer and more uncertain road events, demonstrating her adaptability to many competition formats.

Success in Three Events at the 2020 Tokyo Olympics

One of the most amazing feats of versatility in modern Olympic history is Hassan's ability to compete in three difficult events at the Tokyo 2020 Olympics: the 1,500 meters, 5,000 meters, and 10,000 meters. He medaled in all three events, winning gold in the 5,000 and 10,000 meters and bronze in the 1,500 meters.

She demonstrated her ability to recover fast and adapt to the unique challenges of each race by competing in three different events, each of which required a different combination of speed, endurance, and strategies.

Global Records for a Range of Events

Hassan currently holds or has held world records in several different events with wildly varying distances and tempos:

Mile World Record (4:12.33, 2019): This middle-distance competition calls for lightning-fast acceleration and a powerful final burst.

One-Hour World Record (18,930 meters, 2020): This long-distance competition emphasizes mental toughness and endurance because the objective is to run the farthest distance in an hour.

5,000 meters (14:22.12, 2021): Although her world record was eventually surpassed, this race necessitated the endurance and speed balance typical of lengthier track competitions.

Few athletes can equal her ability to perform well at the highest speeds and greatest distances, as seen by her world records.

Success in the Marathon

Hassan's victory in her first-ever marathon, the 2023 London Marathon, was a crucial indicator of her adaptability. Compared to her most well-known track events, the marathon is a whole different race that calls for distinct preparation, mental toughness, and race strategy. She overcame obstacles during the race, such as a side stitch, and finished first in an amazing 2:18:33.

She then demonstrated her ability to move to the longest distances at the greatest level of competition with a second-place result in the 2023 Chicago Marathon in a time that is among the fastest ever recorded, 2:13:44.

Both Mental and Physical Power

Hassan's capacity to withstand the psychological and physical strain of participating in several disciplines in a short period, as she did during the Tokyo Olympics, is what sets her flexibility apart. As crucial as her physical prowess is her mental toughness, which enables her to modify her pace and racing plan for every distinct race.

Versatility in Tactics

An essential element of Hassan's success is her capacity to read races and modify her strategy mid-race:

She has demonstrated the ability to wait patiently in the pack and deliver a potent finishing kick in shorter events, such as the 1,500 meters.

She can start off quickly in lengthier races like the half marathon or 10,000 meters, or she can tactically save energy to make a move in the last few laps or kilometers.

She has dominated a variety of events and distances thanks to her tactical acumen and adaptability as a runner.

An Uncommon Ability

Sifan An unusual quality in the world of distance running is Hassan's versatility. While most athletes focus on either middle-distance or long-distance competitions, Hassan stands out for her ability to excel in both. Her contests range from 1,500 meters to the marathon. She has made history in a variety of events and forms thanks to her unique combination of speed, endurance, tactical awareness, and mental toughness, making her one of the best athletes in contemporary track and field.

Success in Middle-Distance Races (1500m)

Middle-distance races have seen Sifan Hassan's impressive performance, especially in the 1,500 meters, which has been one of her signature events throughout her career. She is among the world's top 1,500-meter runners according to her ability to dominate this event at the highest level of competition thanks to her combination of speed, endurance, and tactical understanding.

Important Results in the 1,500-Meter IAAF Diamond League Title Time for 2015: Sub-4-minute races every time during the season.

As one of the top athletes in this distance, Hassan won the 2015 Diamond League title in the 1,500 meters. She rose to the top of the worldwide rankings by showcasing her consistency and speed in competition against the finest in the world.

2019 IAAF World Championships (Doha): Gold Medal

Time (Championship Record): 3:51.95

At the 2019 World Championships in Doha, Hassan had one of her most memorable performances as she won the gold medal in the 1,500 meters and set a championship record with a time of 3:51.95. Her unprecedented double triumph included this one since she also won the 10,000 meters.

She defeated a very competitive field and recorded one of the fastest times in the event's history, solidifying her position as the sport's dominant power.

Olympic Bronze Medal, Tokyo 2020

Moment: 3:55.86

Despite racing in an intense schedule that included the 5,000 and 10,000 meters, Hassan earned the bronze medal in the 1,500 meters at the Tokyo 2020 Olympics (held in 2021). Considering that she was competing against a new field and had already won two gold medals in longer races, her performance of 3:55.86 was excellent. Her performance showcased her capacity to remain competitive and tough even under great physical and emotional pressure.

Gold Medal at the 2014 European Athletics Championships in the 1,500 meters (4:04.18)

Hassan won her first significant international championship in 2014 when she triumphed in the 1,500 meters at the Zurich European Championships. This was a turning point in her career because it made her a recognized talent in middle-distance running both in Europe and internationally.

Bronze Medal at the 2016 World Indoor Championships in the 1,500 meters

Hassan is also successful indoors; in the 1,500 meters, he took home the bronze medal at the 2016 World Indoor Championships. Her capacity to adjust to various racial situations and yet perform at an exceptional level was demonstrated by her performance.

Strategic Mastery at 1,500 Meters

Hassan is renowned for placing herself intelligently during races, frequently keeping within striking distance of the leaders and using her powerful finishing kick to burst past rivals in the final lap. Her tactical acumen is often what defines her results in the 1,500 meters.

The secret to Hassan's success has been her ability to read the dynamics of the race and act decisively when necessary. She has demonstrated that she can manage both a leisurely tactical race and a fast-paced final.

Combination of Endurance and Speed

Hassan is a master at striking a balance between raw speed and endurance, which are both necessary for the 1,500 meters:

Her speed allows her to race 1,500 meters in under 4 minutes, an elite time only attained by the finest middle-distance runners.

She has trained over longer distances, including the 5,000 and 10,000 meters, so she has the endurance to run a fast pace the entire race without tiring at the finish.

Reliability at the Very Top

What makes Hassan unique is her ability to perform well year-round in regular-season competitions like the Diamond League as well as tournaments. Throughout her career, she has raced several 1,500-meter races in under four minutes, joining the select group of female historical breakers of this record. Sifan Hassan's triumph in the 1,500 meters is evidence of her extraordinary skill, astute tactical judgment, and adaptability as a middle-distance runner. Her domination in this event is demonstrated by her gold medals from the World and European Championships, as well as her bronze from the Olympics in Tokyo. She has been able to succeed in one of the most competitive sports events thanks to her tactical prowess, speed, and endurance.

Success in Long-Distance Races (5000m, 10,000m)

Sifan Hassan's standing as one of the most adaptable and formidable distance runners in contemporary sports has been solidified by her accomplishments in long-distance competitions, especially in the 5,000 and 10,000 meters. Her accomplishments over these two distances demonstrate her tenacity, strategic acumen, and fortitude on a worldwide scale. The main points of her triumph in the 5,000 and 10,000 meters are listed here.

Important Results at the 2019 IAAF World Championships (Doha) 5,000 Meter Gold Medal

The time is 14:26.72.

At the 2019 World Championships in Doha, Hassan completed a historic double by winning the gold medal in the 5,000 meters. She also won the 10,000 meters. Her victory was especially noteworthy since she ran a very strategically sound race, pulling away from the field in the last few laps to establish a comfortable lead and show off her remarkable endurance and finishing speed.

Tokyo 2020 Olympics: Gold Medal (5,000 Meters)

Moment: 14:36.79

Hassan took home the gold in the 5,000 meters at the Tokyo 2020 Olympics, her first of two golds in the competition. Hassan prevailed over an extremely competitive competition thanks to her strong finishing kick in the last 300 meters. This race was a part of her historic triple-event (1,500, 5,000, and 10,000 meters) Olympic challenge in Tokyo.

In the 5,000 meters, the European Record (2021)

The time is 14:22.12.

In 2021, Hassan broke the 5,000-meter European record in a meet held in Hengelo, Netherlands, with a time of 14:22.12. Her position as one of the fastest women in history over this distance was further cemented by her run that broke the record. Hassan's run was among the quickest in the event's history, proving her competitiveness even though Letesenbet Gidey eventually smashed the record.

Important Results in the 10,000-Meter Gold Medal at the 2019 IAAF World Championships in Doha

30:17.62 is the time

At the 2019 World Championships, Hassan won gold in the 10,000 meters, her first major victory in this event, with a time of 30:17.62. She became the first athlete to ever complete the long-distance double at the World Championships with this triumph and her win in the 5,000 meters. Her successful breakout from the pack during the demanding 25-lap 10,000m race demonstrated her endurance and tactical acumen.

Olympic gold medal in the 10,000 meters at Tokyo 2020

29:55.32

During the Tokyo 2020 Olympics, Hassan's gold medal-winning performance in the 10,000 meters was one of her most memorable moments. She showed amazing perseverance to win gold in the 10,000 meters after having already participated in the 1,500 meters (bronze) and 5,000 meters (gold), making history as the first woman to medal in all three events at one Olympics. Her remarkable performance of 29:55.32 was aided by a well-timed sprint in the last lap that allowed her to gain a significant lead over her competitors.

European 10,000-meter record (2021)

29:06.82 is the time.

With a time of 29:06.82 in the 10,000 meters at Hengelo, Netherlands, in June 2021, Hassan set a new European record. She broke the world record with this performance, although it was only held for a short while as Letesenbet Gidey beat it two days later. Even though she didn't win the world record, Hassan's pace is still among the best in 10,000 meters ever and shows off her remarkable long-distance speed and endurance.

Hassan's Approach to Long-Distance Running

Both Speed and Endurance

In both the 5,000 meters and 10,000 meters, Hassan combines tremendous endurance with a remarkable finishing pace. Even at extremely fast speeds, she is renowned for her ability to maintain pace with the lead group and then deliver a devastating kick in the last meters of the race. This ability to close races swiftly has been important to her success in large contests, as she typically defeats competitors who lack her strong finishing kick.

Tactical Intelligence

One of Hassan's best qualities is her tactical approach to long-distance competitions. She frequently conserves energy in the early going of the race by being patient and keeping a close distance from the leaders. She keeps a close eye on the field as the race goes on, timing her last charge just right. Her success in longer races is largely dependent on her ability to read the race dynamics and make timely, intelligent decisions.

Flexibility

Hassan has demonstrated her ability to adjust to running at a fast or slow pace during the race. She has performed exceptionally well in both tactical, slow-starting races where the last few laps are critical and fast races from the gun. Being adaptable enables her to modify her approach based on the course of the race, which is uncommon in long-distance running since most competitors are more focused on developing a fast or tactical style.

Effects of Running Long Distances

The achievement of Sifan Hassan in the 5,000 and 10,000 meters has changed the definition of what it means to be a long-distance runner in the contemporary day. She is among the select few athletes who have triumphed in races spanning from the 1,500 meters to the 10,000 meters, thereby bridging the gap between middle-distance and long-distance competitions. Her record-breaking double in the 2019 World Championships and her three-medal haul at the 2020 Olympics in Tokyo are proof of her extraordinary adaptability, fortitude, and unmatched work ethic.

One of the best distance runners of her generation is Sifan Hassan, thanks to her supremacy in the 5,000 and 10,000 meters. Her triumphs in the Olympic and World Championships, as well as her records in Europe, highlight her exceptional stamina, tactical acumen, and finishing speed. Hassan is a true icon of the long-distance running community because she never stops pushing the envelope, both on the track and on the road.

Balancing Multiple Events in Major Competitions

Sifan Hassan stands out as one of the most exceptional athletes in contemporary track and field because of her ability to balance several disciplines in important tournaments. Her capacity to compete at the greatest level across widely varied distances in a single competition or tournament has surprised the sports world. This adaptability calls for extraordinary physical stamina as well as mental toughness, clever preparation, and cautious recuperation protocols. Key elements of Hassan's strategy for juggling several events in significant tournaments are listed below:

2020 Tokyo Olympics: Triple Event Difficulty

Hassan's remarkable achievement at the Tokyo 2020 Olympics, where she raced in three demanding races—the 1,500 meters, 5,000 meters, and 10,000 meters—and medaled in each, is the most famous illustration of her ability to balance numerous events.

In the 5,000 meters, gold medal

Before her last 1,500-meter race, Hassan competed in a 5,000-meter race. With a time of 14:36.79, she won gold and easily defeated her rivals. Her first gold medal in the Olympics served as a springboard for her multi-event campaign.

Bronze in the 1,500-meter event

Hassan competed in the 1,500 meters after winning the gold in the 5,000 meters. Her performance of 3:55.86 earned her a bronze medal, which was impressive considering the intensity of the competition and the fact that her body was still recuperating from her 5,000-meter race, despite the physically and mentally taxing schedule.

Gold Trophy for 10,000 meters

In the 10,000 meters, Hassan finished with a second gold medal in 29:55.32, capping off an incredible season. Arguably, the 10,000-meter race proved to be her most difficult event due to the physical strain of competing in numerous long-distance races so soon after the 1,500- and 5,000-meter events. Despite these difficulties, she turned in an incredible last lap, blowing past her rivals to win her second gold medal of the Games.

IAAF World Championships 2019: Two wins

Hassan also accomplished a historic double at the 2019 World Championships in Doha, winning the 10,000 meters and the 5,000 meters. Her remarkable endurance and capacity to manage races across two long-distance events made her the first athlete to win gold in both long-distance events at the World Championships.

The 10,000 Meters of Gold

With a pace of 30:17.62, Hassan won the gold medal in the 10,000 meters to start her campaign. In the last circuits, she used a well-timed surge to pull ahead of the pack. With this victory, she proved her strength and endurance—two crucial attributes for her next 5,000-meter race.

The 5,000 Meters of Gold

Following the physically taxing 10,000 meters, Hassan bounced back to win the 5,000 meters in 14:26.72. It took a very disciplined approach to recuperation and energy management in between races in addition to cautious pacing and mental focus to win both events at such a high level in such a short amount of time.

Energy Saving and Tactical Planning

Hassan has demonstrated a remarkable ability to conserve energy and time her efforts to peak during crucial stages of her races in major events. This tactical knowledge is even more crucial when participating in many events:

Positioning for Race: To save energy and accelerate when the pace picks up, Hassan frequently stays in the pack rather than taking the lead early in races. Final Kick: Whether in middle- or long-distance races, her devastating finishing pace has come to define her racing style. It enables her to defeat rivals in the closing stages.

Recuperation and Adaptability

Managing several events calls for both excellent recuperation techniques and a remarkable physical skill set. In various sports, there is frequently little time between heats, semifinals, and finals; hence, Hassan's capacity for rapid recovery is crucial to her success:

Nutrition and Hydration: When competing in back-to-back competitions, athletes like Hassan must maintain adequate diet and hydration. Her ability to compete at such a high level was probably greatly aided by her team's proficiency in recovery techniques.

Mental Hardiness: Hassan's mental toughness is also significant. She has demonstrated the capacity to remain composed and concentrated under duress, especially in championship situations where an athlete's confidence and attention may be affected by competing in several events.

Special Capability to Travel Great Distances

Very few athletes in history have been able to compete at the same level in middle- and long-distance races. Long-distance competitions like the 10,000 meters call for higher endurance and strategic pacing over an extended period, while middle-distance races like the 1,500 meters require more speed and tactical positioning. Hassan's remarkable versatility as a runner is demonstrated by her ability to switch between these several race formats. Each race has distinct physical and mental requirements, and the struggle is increased when one must balance these while taking on new opponents in every event.

Preparing for a Variety of Events

Hassan trains to develop both speed for shorter races, like the 1,500 meters, and endurance for longer races, like the 10,000 meters, to succeed in various competitions. Her education probably consists of:

High Mileage: Developing a robust aerobic foundation to meet the demands of extended-distance competitions.

Work on Speed: To improve her finishing speed in middle-distance events, she does interval training and tempo runs.

Strength training: The process of developing total body strength and endurance to maintain exertion for a short period during several competitions.

Effects on Field and Track

What is feasible for distance runners in important contests has been redefined by Hassan's capacity to manage several tournaments. Her performances in the 2019 World Championships and the Tokyo 2020 Olympics have challenged established limitations in the sport by demonstrating that one athlete can be competitive—and dominant—across distances ranging from 1,500 meters to 10,000 meters.

Sifan Hassan's ability to manage several events at prestigious contests is evidence of her adaptability, tenacity, and mental toughness. She frequently wins several medals at the top levels of the sport, demonstrating her ability to excel in all formats whether competing in middle- or long-distance events. Her tactical racing style, along with her strong physical attributes and efficient recuperation methods, have established her as a unique figure in track and field history.

Chapter 6: Challenges and Comebacks

Sifan Hassan's career has been characterized by noteworthy setbacks and comebacks in addition to amazing victories. Her success as one of the world's most adaptable and resilient athletes has been largely attributed to her capacity to overcome challenges both on and off the track. Here are a few of the biggest obstacles Hassan has had to overcome along the way, along with some amazing comebacks.

Obstacles

1. Setbacks from injuries

Any elite athlete's career will inevitably include injuries, and Hassan is not exempt from them. She struggled with ailments in 2017, which had an impact on how she performed in London at the World Championships. Hassan had to endure a tough time recovering after only finishing in fifth place in the 1,500 meters and second place in the 5,000 meters.

Both Mental and Physical Toll: Running long- and middle-distance races puts a strain on the body, and recovering while attempting to keep form at its best is a never-ending task. Coping with an injury can also be mentally taxing, particularly if rehabilitation is taking a long time.

2. Olympic Postponement in 2020

For Hassan and many other sportsmen, the COVID-19 pandemic's delay of the Tokyo 2020 Olympics presented a special difficulty. Hassan had a significant interruption due to the unpredictability of the Games' schedule and the potential impact of the pandemic on her preparation and competing regimen.

Interruptions to Training: It became challenging to strike the ideal balance between training intensity and recuperation when access to facilities was restricted. An extra year of intensive attention and training for an event she had been aiming for for years was required due to the Olympics' delay.

3. Difficult Competition

Especially in long-distance events, Hassan has regularly faced some of the world's most formidable opponents. Hassan has frequently been pushed to her boundaries by rivals like Letesenbet Gidey, who achieved world records mere days after Hassan did. Kenya also has a robust middle-distance contingent. Her training and tactics have had to change constantly to remain ahead of such talented competitors.

Pressure to Perform: Running several events at major championships puts a lot of pressure on one to continuously deliver excellent performance, particularly when competing against elite fields over various distances.

4. Exhaustion and Planning

Managing several events at big championships has unique difficulties. Specifically, the mental and physical exhaustion from competing in multiple events in a short amount of time is intimidating. Hassan had to juggle the demands of racing in the 1,500, 5,000, and 10,000 meters during the Tokyo 2020 Olympics.

Physical weariness brought on by the short intervals between events might make it challenging to compete at your best in every race. It also wears on the mind to maintain confidence and concentrate throughout a demanding schedule.

Reentry

1. Injury Recuperation (2017-2019)

Despite suffering an injury setback in 2017, Hassan recovered well in the years that followed. Her ability to bounce back from the injury time proved her mental tenacity and will to compete at the highest level once more.

2019's breakthrough: 2019 marked a turning point in Hassan's career after she steadily regained her form in 2018. She accomplished a historic double in Doha, becoming the first athlete in history to win the 1,500 and 10,000 meters at the same IAAF World Championships. This victory, which came after years of arduous training, demonstrated to the world that she was not only capable of overcoming obstacles but also of rising to the top of her discipline.

2. Return Following the 2021 Olympic Postponement

For Hassan, the cancellation of the Olympics in Tokyo 2020 proved to be a godsend. She strengthened her training program and improved her racing strategies with the extra year of preparation. Her achievement in preparing for the rescheduled 2021 Games was demonstrated by her remarkable triple-event campaign in Tokyo.

Tokyo awarded three medals: The highlights of Hassan's comeback were her two gold medals from the Olympics in the 5,000 and 10,000 meters as well as her bronze in the 1,500 meters. Her incredible fortitude and capacity to overcome obstacles were demonstrated by the fact that she competed over such a wide range of distances and nevertheless won medals in each of the three events.

3. Comebacks to World Records

When Hassan broke the world record in the 10,000 meters in June 2021 with a time of 29:06.82, it was one of the most memorable events of her career. Amazingly, Letesenbet Gidey broke her record a mere two days later. Hassan didn't let this discourage her; instead, it inspired her to keep pushing herself to new limits.

Concentrate on Performance: Despite the rapid rotation of records, Hassan remained focused on her performances. Not long after, she returned to the Tokyo Olympics with a newfound determination, winning the 10,000 meters as well as the 5,000 meters, demonstrating that her strength wasn't just in breaking records but also in triumphing when it counted most.

4. Overcoming Tokyo Fatigue

Hassan's remarkable capacity to recuperate in between races at the

Tokyo 2020 Olympics was evident despite the demanding schedule. She placed third in the very competitive and extremely tactical 1,500 meters after taking first place in the 5,000 meters. After that, Hassan completed her Olympic career with a breathtaking victory in the 10,000 meters, earning her second gold medal of the competition with her amazing last-second kick.

Mental fortitude and recuperation: Her ability to recover from the exhaustion of several events is evidence of her intense training and resilience. Hassan's ability to mentally regroup and concentrate on the next task after the physical strain of each race was crucial to her victory in Tokyo.

Emotional and Mental Hardiness

Hassan's mental toughness has been the foundation of her victories despite all of the difficulties she has encountered, including weariness, injuries, the pandemic, and fierce competition. She has consistently shown that she is capable of staying driven and focused even when things are not going her way.

Accepting Setbacks: Hassan has embraced setbacks, like as injuries or losing her world record, by viewing them as teaching moments. She has not only been able to regain her shape but also surpassed her prior achievements because of her persistently pushing herself beyond her comfort zone and maintaining an optimistic outlook.

Competitive Spirit: Hassan's spirit of competition has always encouraged her to get better and adjust, as seen in the way she responds to setbacks or poor performance in races. She has demonstrated her capacity to overcome hardship by coming back stronger each time.

Sifan Hassan's career is a compelling story of overcoming obstacles head-on and pulling off incredible comebacks. She has demonstrated time and time again that she is capable of overcoming challenges, whether it is via injury, the Olympics being postponed, or competing in many events against the top athletes in the world. Her unprecedented successes in major championships, particularly her triple-medal performance in Tokyo, stand as a monument to her resilience, determination, and uncompromising competitive spirit. Hassan's career is an encouraging illustration of how accomplished athletes can overcome adversity to triumph and keep pushing the envelope of what's feasible in sports.

Injuries and Setbacks

Sifan Hassan has experienced his fair share of injuries and setbacks on his path to becoming one of the most renowned distance runners in the world. Hassan, like many other exceptional athletes, has overcome challenges that have tried her resolve, endurance, and willpower on both a mental and physical level. But these difficulties have just highlighted her amazing capacity to overcome setbacks and keep setting new records in the sports world.

Setbacks from injuries

1. Accidents In the 2017 Season

Hassan had a number of difficulties in 2017, one of which was her battle with many injuries. She gained notoriety in the 1,500 meters, however, her performance in the London 2017 World Championships fell short of expectations. She received a silver medal in the 5,000 meters and placed fifth in the 1,500 meters.

Effects of the Injuries: These wounds not only compromised her physical appearance but also interfered with her training, making it harder for her to provide her best. Because she needed time to heal and regain her strength, this setback marked a turning point in her career.

2. Persistent Injury Throughout the Career

Even after 2017, Hassan continued to deal with a number of bothersome injuries, especially considering the intense training needed for middle- and long-distance competitions. Her Achilles and calves have been recurrent injuries, necessitating time away from competition for her to recover and prevent future harm.

Training Modifications: To deal with these injuries, Hassan and her coaching staff have had to alter their training schedule. They have been concentrating on striking a balance between endurance exercises and methods of preventing injuries, like strength training and physical treatment.

3. Recuperation Procedure

After suffering injuries, Hassan frequently had to return to racing gradually and take her time before reaching her peak performance. It has always been difficult to strike a balance between the need to properly recover and the urge to compete. Her recuperation has required patience since pushing herself too hard too soon would have resulted in more difficulties.

Emotional and Mental Difficulties

1. Expectations and Pressure

The demand to constantly deliver at the best level increased as Hassan's career developed and her success increased. Any athlete can experience mental exhaustion from managing such high expectations, and Hassan's desire to participate in numerous disciplines at big championships made it even more difficult.

Mental Fatigue: It takes a tremendous amount of mental toughness to compete in middle- and long-distance events like the 1,500, 5,000, and 10,000 meters. Mental weariness has occasionally resulted from the expectation to compete well in every event and the intense demands of training for several distances.

2. 2020 Olympic Postponement

Hassan also suffered a great deal when the COVID-19 outbreak forced the postponement of the Tokyo 2020

Olympics. She had been preparing hard, like many athletes do, with the Olympics as the main focus, but her plans were derailed by the uncertainty of when they would take place.

Disrupted Routine: The pandemic created an air of uncertainty, interfered with competition schedules, and limited access to training facilities. This was a big task for Hassan, who was getting ready for an unprecedented Olympic triple-event challenge.

Loss of Momentum: She can have a physical and psychological setback as a result of the pause in training and competition. It was a challenging task for her and her staff to remain focused and remain at their best despite such a lengthy and unpredictable wait.

Rebounds from Adversity

1. Return in 2019

Despite his disappointments in 2017, Hassan had one of the greatest comebacks in sports history in 2019. She won the 1,500 and 10,000 meters in the 2019 IAAF World Championships in Doha, creating history in the process after two years of regaining her strength. This was an extraordinary accomplishment that demonstrated her complete recuperation from prior injury setbacks.

Historical Victories: It was an unprecedented achievement for Hassan to win both the long-distance 10,000 meters and the middle-distance 1,500 meters in the same tournament; this demonstrated her perseverance and her capacity to succeed in a variety of sports.

2. Achievement in Tokyo (2021)

When the Olympics finally came around in 2021, Hassan did an amazing job of fulfilling her dream of competing in three different events. She was the first woman to medal in all three distances at an Olympics, taking home gold in the 5,000 meters, bronze in the 10,000 meters, and gold in the 1,500 meters.

Thriving Under Pressure: Hassan returned stronger than ever despite the protracted wait and uncertainty. Her mental and physical toughness was evident in her ability to compete at such a high level in three demanding events in such a short amount of time.

Lessons Discovered from Failures

1. Flexibility and forbearance

Due to her past injuries, Hassan has learned the value of adaptation in her training and patience in her recuperation. Her training load has been adjusted, and she is now more focused on long-term achievement than on returning too soon to competition.

Training Smarter: Hassan has been able to prolong her career and prevent reoccurring injuries that could compromise her performance at major championships by changing her training program to place more emphasis on injury prevention and rehabilitation.

2. Resilience of Mind

Hassan's success can be attributed in large part to the mental toughness she acquired by overcoming obstacles. She is now mentally stronger after overcoming the difficulties of injury, competition pressure, and pandemic uncertainty, which enables her to maintain her motivation and attention even in trying circumstances.

3. Rivalry in Fire

Hassan has embraced her setbacks as inspiration to rise above them and become a stronger person. Her hardships and defeats have strengthened her will to compete, inspiring her to take on new challenges and push the boundaries of her capabilities. Her perseverance in tackling numerous events at the pinnacle, despite the associated physical and emotional difficulties, is clear evidence of this.

Sifan Hassan's career is proof of her tenacity and capacity to transform obstacles into chances for development. Hassan's career could have been destroyed by injuries, mental exhaustion, and pandemic-related setbacks, yet she has continuously bounced back, accomplishing historic achievements like her double gold at the 2019 World Championships and her incredible triple-medal performance at the Tokyo 2020 Olympics. Her story offers an encouraging illustration of tenacity, demonstrating that with enough time, willpower, and confidence in oneself, one can conquer even the most difficult challenges.

Remarkable Comeback Stories

Throughout her career, Sifan Hassan has had several incredible comeback tales that highlight her fortitude, mental toughness, and capacity to overcome obstacles. Her story demonstrates how she has overcome obstacles and come back stronger than before, using setbacks as stepping stones to greater achievement. Below are a few of her most amazing comeback tales:

1. A Season Dogged by Injuries in 2017 to Global Domination in 2019

Hassan's performance declined at the 2017 World Championships in London, when she took home silver in the 5,000 meters and fifth place in the 1,500 meters, following an injury-plagued season. These were disappointing results for a player of her skill, particularly considering that she was battling chronic problems that interfered with her form and training.

2019 saw Hassan's comeback. Over the following two years, she regained her strength and shape, and by 2019, she was back to her best. Her feats that year were one of the most amazing returns in the annals of track & field history:

2019 IAAF World Championships (Doha): Double Gold

Hassan became the first athlete to win gold in both the 1,500 and 10,000 meters during the same championship, making history in both events.

Her performance in the 10,000 meters proved her mettle in long-distance competitions as she won the gold medal in 30:17.62 with a tactically flawless run.

Her dominance in the 1,500-meter and championship record of 3:51.95 just a few days later solidified her status as a top-tier middle-distance runner.

With this historic double triumph, she fully recovered from the 2017 injury setbacks and showed her remarkable adaptability. Hassan's dominance over a variety of distances was cemented at the 2019 World Championships, demonstrating that his failures were only momentary.

2. Moving the 2020 Tokyo Olympics to 2021 Triple Medal Glory

Hassan was not the only athlete affected negatively by the COVID-19 pandemic-related postponement of the Tokyo 2020 Olympics. She had previously set high standards for herself at the Games, wanting to compete in three different events (the 1,500, 5,000, and 10,000 meters), thus the delay raised doubts about her ability to stay at her best for the duration of her preparation.

Return in 2021

Upon the final holding of the Tokyo Olympics in 2021, Hassan accomplished one of the most remarkable reversals in contemporary Olympic history:

The 5,000 Meters of Gold

With a timing of 14:36.79 in the 5,000 meters, Hassan won gold to start her Olympic career and became the clear favorite in a number of races.

In the 1,500 meters, bronze

Hassan participated in the 1,500 meters and took home a bronze medal after winning the gold in the 5,000 meters. She was tired from competing in so many events, but she showed resiliency by performing well against new opponents.

The 10,000 Meters of Gold

After competing in the 10,000 meters, Hassan finished her Olympic career in

29:55.32 to win gold. Her reputation as one of the most adaptable and resilient competitors in track and field history was solidified with this final triumph.

Her incredible narrative of mental and physical perseverance is demonstrated by her ability to bounce back from the uncertainty and disruption brought on by the epidemic and yet achieve her goals at the postponed Olympics.

3. Global Record Setbacks and 2021 Resilience

With a time of 29:06.82 in June 2021, right before the Olympics in Tokyo, Hassan broke the previous world mark in the 10,000 meters. But Letesenbet Gidey, her opponent from Ethiopia, smashed her record after just two days, running 29:01.03.

Losing a world record so fast could be discouraging for many athletes, but Hassan turned it into fuel for her performance in the Olympics in Tokyo, which was only a few weeks away.

Return at the 2021 Tokyo Olympics

Rather than wallow in her disappointment about losing her world record, Hassan focused her energies on getting ready for her Olympic triple-event quest. Her success at the Games, when she won two gold medals and a bronze—a feat no one else in history had accomplished over such distances—was largely due to her ability to maintain mental focus in the face of adversity.

This inspirational tale highlights Hassan's resilience in the face of disappointment about missing out on a world record. She demonstrated that although records come and go, her real priority was succeeding when it counted most.

4. Autumn In the 1,500-meter heat at the 2020 Tokyo Olympics

Hassan experienced a particularly dramatic moment during the 1,500-meter Olympic heats in Tokyo 2020. About 400 meters into the race, she collided with another runner and stumbled, falling. A fall like that would usually signal an end to an athlete's prospects of winning the race.

Return Among the Race

With incredible tenacity, Hassan got back up and raced through the pack, passing every competitor ahead of her to take first place in the heat. Her incredible comeback astounded the sports community and proved her perseverance and mental fortitude.

First Place Finish in the Heat

Hassan placed first in her heat despite falling, guaranteeing her place in the 1,500-meter semifinals.

Bronze in the 1,500-meter event

Following his recovery from the fall, Hassan won a bronze medal in the 1,500-meter event. Her fall and recovery from it became one of the most talked-about events of the Tokyo Games, illustrating her fortitude and will to compete.

5. Setbacks and Silver Medals on the Path to Dominant Victory

Hassan's evolution as a competitor was impacted by her experiences with setbacks early in her career. She placed third in the 1,500 meters but took home silver in the 5,000 meters at the 2017 World Championships. Even though these defeats were devastating, Hassan learned from them and was motivated to improve her race tactics and stamina.

Return as the World Champion

She had an extraordinary reaction to these disappointments. Hassan had become a dominant force over a variety of distances by the time of the 2019 World Championships and the 2021 Tokyo Olympics, taking home numerous gold medals and setting world marks. Her perseverance and development are evident in her capacity to bounce back from early setbacks and establish herself as a consistent champion at the greatest level.

Throughout her career, Sifan Hassan has accumulated several motivational comeback tales that demonstrate her tenacity, bravery, and refusal to allow failures to define who she is. Hassan has demonstrated time and time again that she is capable of conquering any obstacle. Examples include recovering from injuries sustained in 2017 to win numerous world titles in 2019, winning three medals in 2021 despite the disruption caused by the Olympic postponement, and qualifying for the semifinals after falling during a race. Not only has she recovered physically, but her comebacks are also a testament to her amazing ability to maintain mental focus, overcome obstacles, and emerge stronger each time.

Chapter 7: Training and Coaching

In addition to her natural ability, Sifan Hassan's outstanding accomplishment as one of the top distance runners in the world can be linked to the intense, focused training and guidance she has received over the years. Her successful journey to several world records and Olympic medals has been attributed to her great relationship with her coaches, her dedication to both physical and mental development, and her tough training regimes.

Important Training Guidelines

Flexibility in Instruction

Hassan's ability to compete at the highest level in both middle-distance (1,500 meters) and long-distance events (5,000 meters, 10,000 meters) is one of the distinctive features of her training.

This necessitates a thoroughly thought-out training program that takes into account the various requirements of each event:

The main goals of middle-distance training are anaerobic capacity, speed, and tactical race plans.

Pacing, aerobic conditioning, and endurance are the main focus of long-distance training.

Her adaptability and success in a variety of situations have been greatly attributed to her capacity to transition between these various strategies.

High-Intensity Endurance Exercise

Hassan's training, like that of many other elite distance runners, is based on logging large amounts of mileage; during peak training periods, he frequently logs between 100 and 120 miles per week. By doing this, she strengthens her base of endurance and can run faster over greater distances. To keep her competitive in shorter races, it's important to strike a balance between this and speedwork.

Speed Work and Interval Training

Hassan needs to perform well in speed sessions, like interval training, to succeed in middle-distance races like the 1,500 meters. These exercises frequently consist of short recovery intervals between consecutive sprints to increase lactic threshold, anaerobic capacity, and finishing speed. She can sustain her fastest speed during the crucial last laps of a race thanks to this kind of training.

Climbing Hills and Building Muscle

Hassan's regimen includes hill training as a crucial component to assist him develop his strength, speed, endurance, and resilience. Hassan gains the strength required to kick at the finish line of competitions and enhances her running economy—a critical skill for middle and long distance running—by including hills into her training regimen.

Concentrate on Healing

Hassan trains at a high volume and intensity, so recovery is a crucial component of her routine. This comprises:

Sessions of physical treatment to avoid injuries.

Conditioning and strength to increase the resilience of muscles.

She allowed her body to heal between strenuous sessions with planned rest days and short recovery runs.

Mentoring and Coaching

1. The Nike Oregon Project with Alberto Salazar (2016-2019)

From 2016 until 2019, Sifan Hassan participated in the contentious Nike Oregon Project, which was led by renowned coach Alberto Salazar. She made quick growth and progress during this time, especially in her capacity to race over longer distances and 1,500 meters.

Structured Training Methods: Salazar, renowned for his rigorous and extremely scientific training methods, assisted Hassan in making strides in her endurance, speed, and racing strategy. She developed greater skills in handling the tactical difficulties of important competitions under his direction, and her performance started to significantly increase.

Training Intensity: Particular interval training plans and high-altitude training camps were highly valued components of the Oregon Project. Her achievements, such as the world records she achieved and the victories she had at the

European Championship, were largely due to this methodical approach.

Change Following Salazar's Ban: Due to doping infractions, Salazar received a four-year suspension in 2019 and the Nike Oregon Project was dissolved. The change was a pivotal point in Hassan's career even if she was not found guilty of anything. Hassan didn't lose focus in the face of the upheaval, and she soon went on to work with other instructors to keep up her progress toward global and Olympic achievement.

2. The Post-Oregon Project's Tim Rowberry

Following the Oregon Project's breakup, Hassan teamed up with Tim Rowberry, Salazar's assistant coach. Hassan's following chapter in her career, which included her gold medal wins at the 2019 IAAF World Championships and her incredible exploits at the Tokyo 2020

Olympics, was greatly aided by Rowberry.

Continuity of Training: Rowberry kept up many of the fundamentals of the training she had been receiving from Salazar, especially her high mileage and strength-training regimens. But he also added fresh components to help her hone her strategies and mentally get ready for important occasions.

Mental Preparation: Rowberry worked with Hassan to strengthen her race strategy and mental toughness, which will help her perform at her best in high-stakes events like the Tokyo Olympics. Hassan's ability to stay composed and focused under pressure is one of her distinguishing traits.

Mental Preparedness and Adaptability

Managing Stress and Exhaustion

Hassan's training has produced remarkable results, one of which is her capacity to withstand the mental strain and physical exhaustion associated with competing in numerous events at major championships. Her mental readiness, which keeps her competitive and focused in tough situations, is just as important as her physical training.

Her mental toughness is supported by the following strategies: Visualization to get ready for races and for obstacles.

Practicing mindfulness and meditation can help you stay focused and reduce anxiety before races.

Adaptability and Race Strategy

Hassan's ability to carry out tactical racing strategy is another factor in her success, especially in events like the 1,500 meters when finishing speed, location, and pace are crucial. She has been working with her coaches to improve her ability to read the race and know when to move, particularly in the championship finals when the opposition is fierce.

She won the 1,500-meter heat in Tokyo by immediately getting back up after falling, demonstrating her ability to adjust in the middle of a race. This is evidence of both her mental and physical toughness.

Altitude Training Environment of Instruction

Hassan frequently trains at high elevations, especially in Iten, Kenya, and Flagstaff, Arizona. Her ability to carry oxygen is increased with altitude training, which also increases her stamina and aerobic endurance. This is especially crucial for her results in longer races, like the 10,000 and 5,000 meters.

Camps for Training

Hassan regularly goes to intense training camps with her trainers prior to big tournaments so she can concentrate entirely on her performance without outside distractions. These camps provide a regulated setting in which every facet of her preparation—diet, recuperation, and mental training—is carefully thought out and carried out.

Sifan Hassan's development into one of the best distance runners in history has been largely attributed to her training and coaching experiences. She has excelled over a variety of distances because of her training, which combines high-mileage endurance work, speed, strength conditioning, and mental preparation. With the help of trainers such as Tim Rowberry and Alberto Salazar, she has customized her training to meet her specific objectives, which include competing in several events at major championships. She is one of the most adaptable and resilient athletes in track and field because of her dedication to her recovery and mental toughness as well as her capacity to consistently push her physical boundaries.

Coaches and Mentors

Sifan Hassan's incredible distance running career has been greatly influenced by her coaches and mentors, whose advice has been crucial to her growth as a top athlete. Their impact extends to mental preparation, race plans, training methods, and career management in general. An outline of the major players throughout Hassan's coaching career is provided below:

1. From 2016 to 2019, Alberto Salazar

Alberto Salazar, a prominent coach recognized for his scientific approach to training and developing great distance runners, was Sifan Hassan's coach when she started her professional career.

Salazar was the head coach of the Nike Oregon Project when she joined.

Impact and Input

High-Performance Training: Salazar acquainted Hassan with an extremely regimented training regimen that prioritized speed work, high mileage, and strength training. His rigorous training regimen set the foundation for her future achievements.

Race Strategy & Tactics: By assisting Hassan in honing her strategies, Salazar helped her get ready for the rigors of both intermediate and long-distance competitions. His background as a top runner gave him the ability to offer insightful commentary on race tactics.

Mental Toughness: By stressing the value of mental toughness and concentration during competitions, Salazar assisted Hassan in developing a strong competitive mindset. She demonstrated this mental toughness in her performances in important competitions.

Change and Effect

Hassan came out of this period with notable results, notably her breakout performances in the 2019 IAAF World Championships, where she won gold in both the 1,500 and 10,000 meters, despite the controversies surrounding Salazar, including his ban for doping breaches in 2019.

2. Tim Rowberry (as of 2019)

Following the Nike Oregon Project's breakup, Hassan teamed up with Tim Rowberry, Salazar's assistant coach. Rowberry took over Hassan's coaching duties and has been instrumental in her development ever since.

Mentoring Philosophies and Accomplishments

Continuity in Training: With an emphasis on her high mileage and interval training, Rowberry stuck to many of the fundamental training concepts that Hassan had established with Salazar. She was able to maintain her peak performance amid a professional shift because of her constancy.

Adaptation and Strategy: As Hassan got ready for the Tokyo 2020 Olympics, Rowberry added additional training components to help her hone her racing tactics. She was able to succeed in her triple-event challenge because of his work with her on race strategy and mental training.

Olympic Success: With Rowberry's coaching, Hassan excelled in the 5,000 and 10,000 meters and took home a bronze in the 1,500 meters, achieving remarkable success at the Tokyo 2020

Olympics. This accomplishment demonstrated how well they worked together and cemented Rowberry's place in her training program.

3. Strategists and Partner Training

Hassan has profited from the assistance of other training partners and strategists in her training environment in addition to her main teachers. Her growth has been greatly aided by training with other top athletes:

Training Groups: She has access to competitive training sessions with other elite distance runners, which has pushed her to raise her game. These settings promote accountability and camaraderie, which are crucial for elite-level training.

Peer mentoring: Hassan has had the opportunity to pick up tips from other athletes, including their training regimens and tactics for competing. Her comprehension of the sport has grown significantly as a result of this peer support.

4. Sports psychologists and mental coaches

Hassan may have worked with mental coaches and sports psychologists to improve her mental training, which is essential for winning in high-stakes events. A crucial component of top athlete preparation is mental coaching, even though individual names might not be made public.

Training for Mental Resilience: Goal-setting, mindfulness, and visualization are a few strategies that can help athletes control their anxiety and perform well under duress. Hassan's ability to stay calm under tough situations, like recovering from a fall during the 1,500-meter heats at the

Tokyo Olympics, demonstrates her mental preparation.

Sifan Hassan's instructors and mentors had a big impact on her path to becoming one of the best distance runners in history. Alberto Salazar provided the framework for her development, while Tim Rowberry has continued to build on that success, helping her through a transitional chapter in her career. Her competitive edge and resilience have been further enhanced with the assistance of mental coaches and training partners. Collectively, these individuals have been instrumental in molding Hassan's extraordinary aptitude and accomplishments in the international arena.

Training Regimen and Strategy

Sifan Hassan has a meticulously planned training schedule and strategy to optimize her performance in both long-distance (5,000 and 10,000 meters) and middle-distance (1,500 meters) competitions. Her training allows her to thrive in a variety of sports by combining high-volume mileage, speed work, strength conditioning, and tactical preparations. An outline of her training schedule and tactics is provided below:

1. Foundational Exercise and stamina

Elevated Miles

Weekly Mileage: Hassan usually runs between 100 and 120 miles a week during his peak training times. For endurance events, a solid aerobic basis is developed through this high-volume method.

Lengthy Runs: Usually lasting between 12 and 20 miles, Hassan incorporates lengthy runs within her weekly routine. She gains more endurance and running economy from these runs.

Time Division

Phased Training: Prioritizing the development of endurance before focusing on speed work and tapering before important contests, Hassan's training is generally organized into phases. Her peak occurs at the appropriate time for important events because of this periodization.

2. Interval training and speed training

Interval Training

Workouts for Speed and Endurance: Hassan uses interval training, which consists of short recovery intervals between consecutive sprints at a race pace. She may, for example, run 1,000-meter repeats at her goal race pace to build the speed endurance needed for middle-distance competitions.

Fartlek Runs: By running at different speeds for varied intervals, she can increase her anaerobic capacity and learn to adjust to shifting race paces.

Sessions of Tactical Speed

Final Kick Training: She trains surges and sprints throughout the last 200–400 meters of her workouts, replicating race conditions, to strengthen her finishing pace.

3. Power and Exercise

Weightlifting

Strength Training: To improve the tenacity and power of her muscles, Hassan incorporates strength training into her routine. Exercises like deadlifts, squats, and core exercises that concentrate on functional strength that leads to improved running performance may be a part of this.

Repeats of Hill Training: Running up hills strengthens her legs and improves her speed and power. These training sessions help her run more efficiently and get ready for the different terrain that competitions provide.

4. Techniques for Recuperation and Injury Prevention

Days of Active Recovery: Hassan recognizes the importance of recovery and uses lighter training days to combine cross-training exercises like swimming or cycling with moderate runs to speed up recovery without going overboard.

Massage and physiotherapy

Frequent Physiotherapy: She uses methods like massage and myofascial release to preserve muscle health while managing any tightness or possible injuries with the help of physiotherapists.

Sleep and Rest

Hassan places a high value on relaxation and sleep since he understands that proper recuperation is necessary for optimal performance. Ensuring restful sleep every night and planning well-timed rest days are part of this.

5. Strategy and Tactics for Racing

Simulated Racing

Practice Races: Hassan frequently uses race simulations in her training sessions before competitions, which gives her the chance to hone her tactical decision-making, positioning, and pacing skills. Her ability to successfully implement her race plans during actual events depends on this preparation.

The Awareness of Tactical

Understanding the Race: Hassan is renowned for her aptitude for analyzing races and timing her tactical movements. She practices anticipating what her rivals will do and positioning herself strategically so that when the tempo picks up, she can react accordingly.

6. Concentration and Mental Training

Mental Resilience Visualization Techniques: When under duress, especially in races, Hassan uses visualization techniques to picture herself finishing. She feels less nervous and more confident as a result of this mental practice.

Meditation and Mindfulness

Mindfulness Practices: She can stay focused and composed during races by practicing mindfulness and meditation. This helps her stay in the moment and avoid becoming overwhelmed by the competition.

Strength training, focused speed work, high-volume endurance training, and mental preparation are all meticulously combined in Sifan Hassan's training plan. Her tactical awareness during races and her strict attitude to training have allowed her to excel in both middle-distance and long-distance competitions. Hassan has made a name for herself as one of the best athletes in the world by consistently pushing herself to reach amazing achievements in track and field through a combination of mental and physical preparation.

Chapter 8: Personal Life

Sifan Hassan's personal life sheds light on the person behind the achievements, even if her incredible athletic career frequently takes center stage. Her identity as an athlete and a person is shaped by her upbringing, passions, and ideals.

1. Background and Early Life

Birthplace: Asmara, Eritrea was the birthplace of Sifan Hassan on January 1, 1993. Her early years were spent in a nation with a vibrant culture and a turbulent political climate.

Arrival in the Netherlands: At the age of 15, Hassan left Eritrea for the Netherlands in quest of better prospects and to avoid the unstable circumstances there. She had to adjust to a new environment, language, and culture, so the shift was tremendous.

2. Dutch daily life

Integration into Dutch Society: Hassan had to overcome the difficulties of assimilating into a new society while preserving her cultural identity after relocating to the Netherlands. She pursued her schooling in addition to her sports goals and learned Dutch.

Athletic Development: Middle-distance running was Hassan's first focus when she started her athletic career in the Netherlands. Her growth as an athlete was greatly aided by the resources and encouraging atmosphere found in the Netherlands.

3. Relationships and Family

Family Support: Throughout her struggle, Hassan has received support from her family. Despite her tendency to prioritize her work, she cherishes her relationships with her family and regularly expresses her thanks for what they have given up to allow her to follow her aspirations.

Close Friends: Hassan has forged close bonds with coaches and other athletes, forming a network of support that eases the pressures of high-level competition.

4. Hobbies and Interests

Interests in Culture: Sifan Hassan is deeply rooted in her Eritrean culture. She frequently expresses her pride in her heritage by sharing facets of her culture, such as music, cuisine, and customs.

Travel: Hassan travels widely for contests all around the world as a professional athlete. Making the most of her experiences as an athlete, she frequently travels and investigates the local way of life and tourist attractions.

Community Involvement: Hassan is well-known for her generosity and frequently takes part in programs designed to motivate young athletes, especially those with immigrant families. She encourages young people to follow their goals in sports and education by using her platform.

5. Difficulties and Fortitude

Overcoming Adversity: Resilience and tenacity are hallmarks of Hassan's journey from Eritrea to the status of an elite athlete. Throughout her athletic career, she has encountered several difficulties, such as cultural differences, language hurdles, and the weight of great expectations.

Mental Health Awareness: Hassan has discussed the value of mental health in athletics and emphasized the necessity for players to put their own health first. She aims to spread a positive mindset among her fellow athletes and promotes candid conversations about mental health issues.

6. Social Media Presence Fan Engagement: Sifan Hassan shares details about her training, tournaments, and personal life with her fans and followers on social media channels. Many find her relatability and sincerity appealing, which enables them to establish a personal connection with her.

Inspiration & Motivation: Hassan frequently provides inspirational quotes in her postings and exhorts others to follow their goals. She focuses on the value of tenacity and hard work in particular.

A combination of resiliency, cultural pride, and a dedication to success as an athlete and a person may be seen in Sifan Hassan's personal life. Her path from Eritrea to the top of the international distance running rankings is evidence of her tenacity and perseverance. Hassan continues to inspire many people both on and off the track with her strong familial ties, her passion for culture and travel, and her support of mental health.

Early Life in Ethiopia

Before relocating to the Netherlands, Sifan Hassan's early experiences and Ethiopian roots define her early life. Here's a detailed look at this important part of her life:

1. Origin and History

Sifan Hassan was born in Asmara, Eritrea, on January 1, 1993.

Ethnic background: Despite being born in Eritrea, Hassan is descended from Ethiopia, a fact about which she has frequently expressed pride. The significance of her family's ties to Ethiopia lies in their influence on her upbringing and sense of cultural identity.

2. Growing up in Eritrea

Early Years: Hassan spent her early life in Eritrea, where she was surrounded by a diverse cultural environment. Her resilience, determination, and personality were greatly influenced by her experiences in Eritrea.

Home Life: She was raised in a hardworking, supportive home that emphasized education. Her parents' principles would later shape her outlook on life in general and athletics in particular.

3. The Political Environment and Migration

Political Unrest: Since gaining its independence from Ethiopia in 1993, Eritrea has experienced political unrest and violence. Many families, like Hassan's, were impacted by the difficult political climate, which made them look for better prospects elsewhere.

Migration to the Netherlands: Hassan's family made the difficult decision to leave Eritrea when she was fifteen years old. In an effort to find stability, safety, and better opportunities for the future, they relocated to the Netherlands. She had to adjust to a new environment and culture during this shift, which was a major turning point in her life.

4. Adaptation to Culture

Getting Used to Life in the Netherlands: Hassan had to overcome several obstacles to fully integrate into a new society after moving to the Netherlands, such as picking up the language and adjusting to a new educational system. This encounter demanded tenacity and adaptability, skills that would serve her well throughout her athletic career.

Creating a Community: During Hassan's initial days in the Netherlands, she met other immigrants, formed a new support system, and eventually figured out where she fit into Dutch society.

5. Beginning Sports Activities

Introduction to Running: In the Netherlands, Hassan started taking part in local track and field competitions after realizing she had a knack for running. As she trained and competed, her love for sports developed, and she eventually decided to take distance running more seriously.

Support from Coaches: Her early coaches saw her potential and pushed her to practice hard, giving her the direction she needed to hone her middle-distance running abilities.

6. Effect on Her Personality

Cultural Pride: Hassan has remained deeply rooted in her Ethiopian heritage even after moving. She frequently thinks back on her upbringing and the lessons she received from it, highlighting the significance of grit, determination, and cultural identity.

Inspiration for Others: Many people, especially young athletes from immigrant backgrounds, find inspiration in Hassan's journey from Eritrea to become a great athlete. She is a living example of resiliency and dedication, demonstrating that one can succeed no matter what obstacles they face.

Sifan Hassan's journey as an elite athlete was shaped by her early life in Ethiopia and her subsequent migration to the Netherlands. Her love of running and the difficulties she had adjusting to a new environment and culture set the groundwork for her future achievements on the track. Her tale inspires people throughout the world as a monument to tenacity and the strength of willpower.

Immigration to the Netherlands

Sifan Hassan's road to becoming an elite athlete began with her immigration to the Netherlands, which was a pivotal milestone in her life. This is a thorough synopsis of her experience and how it affected her career:

1. The Cause of Immigration

Leaving Eritrea: Hassan's family left Eritrea in search of safety and better prospects overseas. They were born and reared there, during a period of political upheaval and conflict. Their decision to depart was impacted by the challenging circumstances in Eritrea, which included political unrest, extreme poverty, and few opportunities for youth.

Go to the Netherlands: Hassan moved there as a refugee when he was 15 years old. This significant life transition required her to start over in an entirely new setting, leaving behind her home, family, and familiar surroundings.

2. Difficulties in Getting Used to a New Life

Acquiring Fluency in a New Language: Acquiring Dutch was among the most pressing difficulties Hassan had. Resilience and persistence were needed while attending school to adjust to a new language and culture.

Cultural Adjustment: In addition to learning the language, she also had to get used to Dutch social and cultural conventions, which were very different from her upbringing in Eritrea. The dual experiences of immigration and refugee status contributed additional intricacies to her process of adapting.

Education and Support from the Community: Hassan continued her studies in the Netherlands while simultaneously becoming a part of her neighborhood. The nation's refugee support networks assisted her in acclimating to her new life by offering support for integration initiatives and language acquisition.

3. The Finding of Running

Overview of Athletics: Hassan first started jogging as a hobby in the Netherlands to keep in shape. Still, her innate ability was soon recognized, and she soon started competing in nearby track meets. She was able to develop her skills because of the Dutch sporting system's structured setting.

Assistance from Mentors and Coaches: When she began competing in running competitions, local coaches noticed her potential. Her professional running career began when she was mentored and inspired to pursue competitive athletics.

4. Making the Switch to Competitive Running

Joining a Running Club: Hassan became a member of a nearby running club, where she had her first official training session. Her technique and endurance were enhanced by the coaching she received from seasoned instructors and her exposure to elite racing in Europe.

Quick Progress: She made quick progress in her running. She began competing in the Netherlands at the national level in a matter of years. Hassan had become one of the nation's best runners by 2013 after taking first place in national cross-country and track competitions.

5. Dutch Nationality and Participation

Getting Dutch Citizenship: In 2013, Hassan obtained Dutch citizenship, enabling her to compete internationally on behalf of the Netherlands. For her, this was a momentous occasion because it strengthened her ties to her new country and provided her with the chance to participate internationally.

First International Success: Representing the Netherlands, Hassan made her breakthrough in 2014 at the European Athletics Championships in Zurich, where she won the 1,500 meters and secured her first significant international victory.

6. Identity as an Immigrant and Athlete Pride in Dual Heritage: Hassan is proud of her Ethiopian and Eritrean ancestry even if she has completely embraced her Dutch identity. She discusses her struggles as a refugee and how they influenced her will to succeed frequently.

Motivating Others: The story of Hassan's transformation from a child refugee to an Olympic winner is one of tenacity, resiliency, and diligence. Many people are inspired by her tale, particularly immigrants and refugees, who view her as an example of how to overcome hardship and prosper in a foreign land.

A significant turning point in Sifan Hassan's life was her immigration to the Netherlands, which also signaled the start of her amazing athletic career. She became one of the world's best distance runners after focusing her energies on running despite the difficulties of adjusting to a new nation, way of life, and language. Her narrative serves as an example of both the human spirit's resiliency and the transforming potential of athletics.

Balancing Athletics with Personal Life

Elite athletes like Sifan Hassan face difficulty in juggling the demands of rigorous training and competition schedules while preserving their connections, physical health, and emotional well-being. This is how Hassan maintains this equilibrium:

1. Extensive Training Program vs. Self-Demanding Training Plan: Hassan follows an extremely rigorous training program that consists of daily workouts that involve strength training, speed work, long runs, and recovery exercises. It can be challenging to strike a balance between her personal life and her performance concentration because it demands sacrifice and dedication.

Choosing a Rest Period: Recuperation and rest are essential to preserving optimum physical health. Hassan places a high value on sleep to maximize her physical performance as well as to make sure she has time for leisure, socializing, and personal pursuits.

2. Relationships and Social Life

Support System: Hassan's ability to handle the demands of professional athletics is greatly influenced by her close friends, family, and coaches. She has a busy schedule and little time for socializing, but she stays grounded since she has good relationships with her support system.

Athlete Community: Hassan's social life and sports endeavors frequently collide. During training camps and events, she spends time with other athletes, fostering a sense of camaraderie and understanding with those who encounter comparable difficulties in juggling life and sports.

3. Welfare and Mental Health

Prioritize Mental Resilience: Hassan recognizes the importance of mental health and believes that having a positive outlook is crucial for juggling her hectic profession and personal life. To maintain her mental toughness and prevent fatigue, she engages in mindfulness and visualization exercises. Personal pastimes and interests: When she's not racing, Hassan likes to relax with simple things like music, traveling to different countries, and reconnecting with her Ethiopian and Eritrean roots. These pursuits offer a psychological reprieve from the demands of competitiveness.

4. Personal Space and Public Life

Sustaining Privacy: Being a well-known athlete, Hassan is frequently in the spotlight, which can make it challenging to lead a quiet existence. She does, however, exercise great care in maintaining her public persona, striking a balance between media appearances and her wish to keep some details of her private life secret.

Interacting with followers: Hassan takes pleasure in interacting with her followers on social media, offering them glimpses into her training regimen and private life while upholding boundaries that let her concentrate on her professional and well-being.

5. Cultural Identity and Relationships with Family

Strong ties to heritage: Hassan has strong ties to her Ethiopian and Eritrean ancestry even if she now resides in the Netherlands. She finds strength in her ethnic identity, and her family relationships are essential to keeping her emotionally supported and connected to her roots.

Motivation for Newcomers: Hassan's experience as a refugee and immigrant offers her a distinct outlook on life. She makes use of her position to encourage people, especially those from immigrant communities, to follow their dreams in spite of obstacles they might encounter.

6. Goals for the Future and Equilibrium

Long-term Objectives: As Hassan's career develops, it will continue to be important for her to strike a balance between her personal and athletic goals. She strives for success without sacrificing her well-being, whether she is thinking about upcoming competitions or making plans for her post-running life.

Organizing for Life After Athletics: After retiring from professional competition, Hassan has said that she would like to continue mentoring and inspiring upcoming athletes. This demonstrates her progressive attitude to striking a balance between her personal and professional lives.

Sifan Hassan's ability to manage her personal life and sports career is a credit to her perseverance, dedication, and solid support network. Hassan balances her hard career in competitive sports with her home life by putting her mental and physical health first, preserving solid interpersonal bonds, and remaining aware of her cultural background. Her continued performance and general well-being are significantly influenced by this equilibrium.

Chapter 9: Legacy and Influence

Sifan Hassan's impact and legacy go far beyond her amazing on-track accomplishments. Her transformation from a refugee to one of the most accomplished distance runners in the world is a moving example of tenacity, willpower, and the positive effects that sports have on people's lives both locally and globally. Here is a glimpse of the legacy she is creating and her impact on sports and other fields:

1. Dominance in Athletics Over Distance Running Versatility: Hassan's ability to succeed in a variety of races, including the marathon and the 1,500 meters, has changed the definition of what it means to be a distance runner. It is uncommon in the world of sports to see someone excel in both middle- and long-distance

events, but she has demonstrated that it is possible. Her achievements over various distances have raised the bar for what sportsmen may accomplish in their professional lives.

Several World Records: Hassan's accomplishments in the mile and the one-hour run, among others, solidify her status as one of the finest runners in history. Her records serve as a standard for upcoming generations and motivate athletes to pursue excellence.

2. Overcoming Misery

Refugee to Champion: Millions of people worldwide, especially immigrants and refugees, may relate to Hassan's narrative of leaving Eritrea as a youth and going on to win an Olympic medal. Her story is a testament to the strength of tenacity, and her accomplishments offer hope to those who are going through challenging times.

Inspiring Resilience: Throughout her career, Hassan has experienced several setbacks, including injuries and the psychological effects of intense competition. She sets an example for both athletes and non-athletes with her ability to overcome these challenges and bounce back stronger each time, demonstrating both her mental and physical tenacity.

3. Breaking Down Barriers for Women in Sports: Hassan has broken down barriers by being an immigrant and a woman of color in a field where other demographics frequently hold a disproportionate amount of influence. This has encouraged young women from a variety of backgrounds to pursue athletics. She now represents empowerment and proves that one can succeed no matter where they are from.

Hassan is a global role model for young athletes because of her accomplishments in the international arena, as well as her modesty and determination. She keeps inspiring the next generation of runners, especially young girls, by demonstrating to them that hard work and devotion can also lead to greatness.

4. Contribution to the Sport of Running: Thanks to Hassan's accomplishments, distance running has gained more recognition, especially in women's middle- and long-distance competitions. Her spectacular performances have enthralled spectators worldwide, enhancing the reputation of track and field and contributing to the sport's growth.

Pushing Athletic Boundaries: Hassan has pushed the bounds of what athletes can accomplish by competing in numerous events at major championships, such as the Olympics in Tokyo 2020, where she competed in the 1,500, 5,000, and 10,000 meters. This has raised the bar for competition in the sport by motivating others to push themselves to compete in a variety of disciplines.

5. Promoting the Welfare of Athletes and Mental Health

Awareness of Mental Health: Hassan has been candid in discussing the value of athletes' mental health and the pressures and difficulties they encounter. She encourages athletes to put their mental health as much as their physical health first by addressing mental health and lowering the stigma associated with mental health problems in athletics.

Balanced Training Method: Throughout her professional life, Hassan has advocated for a training method that is both balanced and incorporates rest and recovery, thereby bringing attention to the significance of long-term health in sports. Her focus on the value of physical and mental well-being provides a good model for upcoming athletes.

6. Worldwide Impact and Beyond Inspiration from Sports for Immigrants and Refugees: Beyond the realm of sports, Hassan's narrative has a deep emotional connection, especially with immigrant and refugee populations. For those who are experiencing hardship and displacement, she is a potent symbol of hope because she defied the odds to become a global success.

Despite being mainly recognized for her sporting accomplishments, Hassan is dedicated to philanthropy and giving back to her community. She supports programs that encourage young athletes from underrepresented backgrounds and utilize her platform to spread awareness of the difficulties encountered by refugees.

In addition to her world records, Olympic medals, and ground-breaking feats, Sifan Hassan's legacy is shaped by her fortitude, her support of mental health, and her position as a trailblazer for women, refugees, and athletes of color. Millions of people are still motivated by her tale of triumphing over hardship, not just in the sports community but also outside of it. Being one of the most accomplished and adaptable runners in history, Hassan's impact will surely affect distance running going forward and inspire upcoming generations.

Contribution to Women's Distance Running

Sifan Hassan has revolutionized women's distance running by raising the bar for what female competitors can do in middle- and long-distance competitions. Her remarkable accomplishments, adaptability, and capacity to shatter established records have had a long-lasting effect on the sport. Her contributions to women's distance running are as follows:

1. Redefining variety in Distance Running: By dominating events ranging from 1,500 meters to 10,000 meters and even attempting the marathon, Hassan has redefined variety in women's distance running. Her ability to switch between middle- and long-distance events has challenged traditional notions about track and field specialization. Few athletes have been able to dominate over such a broad variety of distances.

Achievement in Major Championships: Hassan has set the bar for women's distance running with her incredible ability to participate in several events at major championships. She proved that women could compete at the highest level in many races and distances at the same time by winning gold in the 5,000 and 10,000 meters at the Tokyo 2020 Olympics and bronze in the 1,500 meters.

2. Shattering World Records: In 2019, Hassan ran a time of 4:12.33 seconds to break the mile record. This demonstrated Hassan's supremacy in middle-distance running and encouraged a new generation of runners to test their boundaries by shattering the previous record held by Svetlana Masterkova in 1996.

One-Hour World Record (2020): In September 2020, Hassan ran 18.930 kilometers to create a new record for the world's longest one-hour race. This accomplishment demonstrated her incredible endurance and solidified her status as one of the sport's most accomplished distance runners.

The Influence of Her Records In addition to securing Hassan's position in women's distance running history, breaking these world records demonstrated that female athletes are capable of pushing the limits of human performance. Young female runners are inspired by her accomplishments and are motivated to pursue greater things in their careers.

3. Exceeding the Competitive Benchmark

Increasing the Bar for Competitiveness: Hassan's accomplishments have raised the bar for women's distance running competition. To meet the standards she has set, athletes are now forcing themselves to compete at an even greater level. Her rivals are motivated to improve their performances by her unwavering will and persistence.

Tactical Brilliance: Hassan has changed the definition of what it means to be a distance runner by using his combination of speed and tactical acumen to win races. She frequently executes well-timed sprints and audacious movements in the closing moments of races, demonstrating that her performances are more than just displays of natural talent. The significance of tactical intelligence in women's middle- and long-distance running has come to light as a result of this.

4. Shattering Gender Barriers and Challenging Conventional Expectations: Hassan's accomplishments have cast doubt on the conventional notions of female athletes, especially those involved in distance running. Hassan has

demonstrated that it is feasible to be competitive throughout a range of distances and in a variety of events, contrary to the historical encouragement for women to specialize in particular sports.

Opening the Door for Future Generations: Hassan has opened the door for upcoming generations of female distance runners to pursue a wide range of challenging professional goals by shattering prejudices about female endurance and versatility. Her accomplishments inspire women to not be constrained by societal expectations but to believe in their ability to thrive in a variety of endeavors.

5. Inspiration and Representation

Role Model for Female Athletes: Hassan is an inspiration to female athletes everywhere, especially to women of color and those who have immigrated or fled their own countries. Her accomplishment demonstrates that women can succeed in sports regardless of their upbringing if they have self-belief, perseverance, and determination.

Encouraging Audiences Worldwide: Beyond the track, Hassan's transformation from a refugee to a professional athlete inspires women and girls everywhere. Her narrative of tenacity and empowerment inspires women to overcome obstacles in all aspect of life, including athletics.

6. Pressing for More Equity and Acknowledgment

Emphasizing Women's Running: Hassan's well-known accomplishments have increased awareness of women's distance running, which has improved the standing and acknowledgment of female track and field athletes. Her world records, Olympic medals, and adaptability as a competitor have increased interest in women's events among spectators and the media, which supports the movement for greater gender parity in sports.

Promoting Women's Sports: Hassan's success in the international arena has aided in the larger push for more media attention, funding, and acknowledgment of women's sports. Her accomplishments have contributed to the challenge of the differences in prize money and recognition between women's and men's sports.

The impact Sifan Hassan has had on women's distance running has been revolutionary. She has revolutionized what is possible in the sport by smashing world records, performing exceptionally well over a variety of distances, and motivating a new wave of female athletes. Her adaptability, spirit of competition, and capacity to defy expectations have elevated the bar for women's sports and solidified her reputation as one of the most significant individuals in distance running history. Hassan's accomplishments and leadership have irrevocably impacted the direction of women's distance running.

Influence on Future Generations of Runners

Sifan Hassan's impact on upcoming running generations is immense and varied, going well beyond her plethora of accomplishments. Her transformation from world champion to refugee, her adaptability across long distances, and her mental toughness have motivated and inspired athletes all over the world. A closer look at how Hassan will continue to impact the upcoming generation of runners is provided below:

1. Broadening the Range of What's Possible Redefining Versatility: Hassan's success in races from 1,500 to 10,000 meters, as well as her first marathon appearance, has broadened the conventional notion of what a distance runner can do. She has challenged young athletes to push themselves in numerous disciplines and break free from specialization by demonstrating that it is possible to excel in a wide range of sports.

Motivating Future Champions: Thanks to Hassan's example, young runners are now more inclined to approach their careers with an open mind, be willing to try different lengths and strive for multi-event success in major championships. Her ability to successfully combine long- and middle-distance running has raised the bar for what other runners should aim for in the future.

2. Shattering Obstacles for Minorities and Women

Representation & Role Model: Hassan's accomplishments as an immigrant and a woman of color inspire young athletes from a variety of backgrounds. She has dismantled boundaries based on race and culture, demonstrating that runners from various backgrounds can be successful on the international scene. Aspiring athletes, especially those from underrepresented populations, find inspiration in her tale, which gives them hope that they may achieve their goals.

Empowering Women in Sports: Hassan's ground-breaking accomplishments have increased awareness of women's distance running, encouraging aspiring athletes to overcome preconceptions and reach new heights. Future generations of female runners will be motivated to push boundaries by her example, as she has demonstrated that women can dominate the sport and compete over a variety of distances.

3. Overcoming Adversity with Resilience and Mental Toughness: Hassan's life story exemplifies resilience. She had to overcome many obstacles to acclimate to life in the Netherlands and further her athletic career after fleeing Eritrea as a refugee. Despite the difficulties, her ascent to the top of the running world offers young runners a model for how to overcome hardship, stay focused, and keep moving forward in the face of difficulties.

Hassan is renowned for her mental toughness, which she uses to compete at the highest level in various competitions and to overcome injuries. She serves as an example for young athletes, showing them that mental toughness is just as important as physical preparation for success in competitive sports.

4. Inspiring Ambition and Confidence Chasing Bold Goals: Future athletes have been motivated to pursue lofty goals by Hassan's daring attempts to compete in numerous Olympic events in Tokyo 2020, where he won gold in the 5,000 and 10,000 meters and bronze in the 1,500 meters. Young runners are inspired by her unwavering quest for excellence to have huge dreams and have faith in their capacity to do amazing things, even if it involves competing in unusual methods.

Stressing Hard Work and Dedication: The running community is aware of Hassan's strong work ethic. Her commitment to training and ongoing development is a shining example of the importance of tenacity and hard effort.

Younger athletes can look up to her as an inspiration for how dedication to one's skill can result in success at the highest levels, and this message strikes a deep chord with them.

5. Novel Approaches to Training and Strategy

Taking a Holistic Approach: Hassan's creative training techniques, which emphasize both mental and physical conditioning, are another factor in her success. Her strategic races, in which she combines endurance, speed, and tactical skill, highlight the value of considering aspects of the sport other than physical ability. Future runners might use similar all-encompassing training methods, emphasizing versatility, race strategy, and mental toughness in addition to pure athleticism.

Tactical Intelligence: Hassan's race tactics highlight the significance of race tactics in distance running. They are frequently characterized by a powerful finish kick or audacious mid-race maneuvers. Future generations will be taught to be astute, flexible competitors on the track by this feature of her racing style, which helps them to develop both endurance and tactical thinking.

6. Dedication to Longevity and Excellence

Longevity in the Sport: Hassan's consistent success throughout the years has established a benchmark for endurance in sports. Future athletes can learn from her ability to balance several events at major championships and retain optimum performance, as she sets an example for how to manage their careers for long-term success. Her career will serve as an example for upcoming runners, showing them that with the correct preparation, perseverance, and flexibility, they too can stay at the top.

Managing Setbacks and Resilience: Despite suffering injuries and setbacks, Hassan has always been able to bounce back stronger. Future runners will be motivated by this resilience, which demonstrates that short-term setbacks are a natural part of the journey and can be overcome with perseverance, the appropriate recovery strategy, and mental focus.

7. Encouraging Equilibrium and Mental Health

Emphasis on Mental Health: Hassan has been transparent about the value of mental health in her professional life and has urged aspiring athletes to place a high priority on their mental health. A new generation of athletes will be influenced by this advocacy to recognize the importance of both mental and physical health practices in achieving long-term success in sports and balancing their training.

Athletics and Life Balance: Hassan's capacity to lead a well-rounded life, remain rooted in her heritage, and discover happiness outside of competition serves as an example for upcoming athletes of the value of balance in attaining long-term success. This message is particularly crucial at a time when young athletes are subjected to growing pressure and expectations.

The impact Sifan Hassan will have on upcoming running generations is immense. Her innovative accomplishments, tenacity, and adaptability have revolutionized the definition of the distance runner. Her narrative encourages young athletes to dream big, overcome obstacles, and pursue excellence in a variety of sports. Women's distance running will continue to be shaped by Hassan's legacy, encouraging upcoming generations to push boundaries and redefine their limits.

Honors and Awards

Throughout her career, Sifan Hassan has won a great deal of recognition for her outstanding accomplishments in middle- and long-distance running, including honors and awards. These honors serve as a testament to her supremacy in the game and her impact on the international scene. An outline of some of her most noteworthy accolades and awards is provided below:

1. Olympic Medals

Olympics Tokyo 2020 (held in 2021)

Gold Medal in 5,000 Meters: Hassan cemented her supremacy in long-distance running by winning the gold in an exciting race.

Gold Medal in the 10,000 meters: With a strong final lap, she won the 10,000 meters to complete her Olympic double.

Bronze Medal in 1,500 meters: Hassan's victory demonstrated her capacity to compete at the greatest level over a variety of distances.

2. Medals from the 2019 IAAF World Championships in Doha

1,500-meter gold medal: Hassan broke the championship record and solidified her domination in the middle distance events by winning the gold medal in the 1,500 meters.

Gold Medal in 10,000 Meters: She was the first athlete to win the 1,500 and 10,000 meters at the same World Championships when she also took home the gold in that event.

3. International Records

World Record in the Mile: In 2019, Hassan broke the 1996 mark by setting a new world record in the women's mile with a timing of 4:12.33.

World Record for One-Hour Run: She ran 18.930 kilometers in an hour in September 2020, setting a new record for the world.

World Record in the 10,000 Meters (June 2021): A few days later, Hassan's time of 29:06.82 briefly held the record for the 10,000 meters.

4. Championships in Europe

2014 European Athletics Championships: Gold Medal in the 1,500 Meter: Hassan became a rising star in European athletics after winning her first significant title in the 1,500 meters.

Bronze Medal in the 1,500 meters at the 2016 European Championships: Hassan achieved another podium result in the 1,500 meters at the European level.

2018 European Championships: Gold Medal in 5,000 Meters: She maintained her reign of supremacy in the European arena by winning the gold medal in the 5,000 meters.

5. Titles in the Diamond League

With several IAAF Diamond League wins under her belt, Hassan has proven her supremacy and consistency across a range of distances, including the 1,500 and 5,000 meters.

6. Dutch Sportswoman of the Year 2014, 2019, 2021: Sifan Hassan received multiple honors as the Dutch Sportswoman of the Year in acknowledgment of her accomplishments across the world and her contribution to the advancement of Dutch sports.

7. A 2022 nominee for the Laureus World Sports Award Nominee for the Laureus World Sports Award: In recognition of

her contributions to the sports industry and her accomplishments at the Tokyo 2020 Olympics, Hassan was put forward for the esteemed Laureus World Sportswoman of the Year award.

8. 2019 European Athlete of the Year: After winning a record double gold at the World Championships in Doha, Hassan was voted 2019 European Athlete of the Year.

9. The nominee for IAAF Athlete of the Year

In recognition of her exceptional achievements on the international front, Hassan has received many nominations for the IAAF Female Athlete of the Year award.

10. Acknowledgment of Social Influence

In addition to her sporting accomplishments, Hassan has received recognition for her inspirational journey as a refugee and her advocacy work on behalf of immigrant and refugee populations using her position as a top athlete.

The accolades and prizes Sifan Hassan has received are a testament to her excellence and versatility as a distance runner. Hassan's achievements on the track are matched by the attention she receives for her tenacity, adaptability, and inspirational tale. She has won gold medals at the Olympics, set world marks, and received national and international honors. Her accolades highlight not only her sporting prowess but also her impact as a worldwide sports legend.

Chapter 10: Future Prospects

Sifan Hassan has a bright future in athletics because of her outstanding accomplishments and unwavering dedication to the game. She is among the world's best middle- and long-distance runners, and several indications point to her being in a strong position to succeed going forward:

1. Persistently High Level of Competition Possibility of Breaking More Records: Hassan has already broken a number of world records, but her tenacity and diligence imply that she might break a few more. She is driven to always improve her competitive nature, and she is likely to set new marks for herself and other top athletes.

Aiming for Big Competitions: Hassan will probably concentrate on defending her championships and possibly increasing her medal total across a range of distances at upcoming competitions like the 2023 World Championships and the 2024 Summer Olympics in Paris.

2. Adaptability Over Distances

Competing in Multiple competitions: What sets Hassan different from many competitors is her ability to compete well in both middle-distance (1,500m) and long-distance (5,000m, 10,000m) competitions. Because of her adaptability, she may plan her training and focus on several activities in important contests, which improves her chances of success and makes her more appealing to sponsors and spectators.

3. Adjustment and Extension

Getting Used to the Marathon: Hassan may decide to pursue marathon running further after her successful switch to larger distances. Given her endurance and tactical racing approach, her expertise with shorter distances may be a benefit in the marathon.

Learning and Developing: Hassan has demonstrated an amazing capacity to take what she has learned from her experiences and modify her approach. Her performance should continue to become better as she participates in more tournaments.

4. Continual Growth, Mental and Physical

Stress on Injury Management: Given Hassan's history of injury-related setbacks, his attitude to training, recuperation, and injury avoidance will be critical. Her tenacity and dedication to preserving her physical well-being will have a big influence on how long she plays the sport.

Mental Fortitude: Hassan's emphasis on mental toughness and readiness will be essential to her success going forward. She may have an advantage over rivals due to her capacity to perform under pressure in important events.

5. Serve as an Advocate and Role Model for Upcoming Generations: Hassan's story can encourage many young athletes to pursue athletics because she is a role model for them, especially for women and athletes from varied backgrounds. Her legacy will be further cemented by her dedication to using her position to promote social causes in addition to her sporting accomplishments.

Participation in Community Initiatives: Her commitment to programs that encourage athletics among marginalized populations and assist young runners may help develop the sport's future athletes and leave a lasting legacy.

6. Brand and Sponsorship Opportunities

Marketability and Sponsorships: Hassan is a sought-after personality for brands and sponsorships due to her rising popularity and achievements. Her popularity will probably make her more marketable, which will improve her financial security and free her up to concentrate more on her preparation and competitive spirit.

7. Extended Career Guidance

Selecting Strategic Events: Hassan's skill at organizing her schedule of competitions will be essential. She can maintain a high level of performance by carefully choosing the events to increase her chances of success and giving herself time to recover.

Thoughts About Retirement Preparations: As Hassan nears the end of her athletic career, she might begin to think about her long-term future, including possible retirement preparations. This can entail going into positions in athletics as a coach, mentor, or advocate.

8. Legacy Construction

Leaving a Legacy: Hassan is doing a great job leaving a long-lasting mark on the sports world. Her accomplishments can raise the bar for upcoming generations of competitors and encourage continued interest in women's distance running.

Sifan Hassan has a promising future in sports thanks to her ability to shatter records, her constant adaptability over long distances, and her influence as a role model. Hassan is well-positioned to continue inspiring athletes worldwide and achieving her own competitive objectives as a prominent figure in distance running for years to come thanks to her excellent work ethic, versatility, and strategic focus.

Upcoming Competitions

With an eye toward major competitions that will provide her the chance to demonstrate her versatility and competence in middle- and long-distance running, Sifan Hassan has an exciting competitive schedule ahead of her. The following are a few of the competitions she is probably going to compete in:

1. The 2024 Summer Olympics in Paris

Dates of the Event: July 26–August 11, 2024

Events: It is anticipated that Hassan will participate in the 1,500, 5,000, and 10,000 meters among other events. Her objectives will be to retain her Olympic championships and possibly win more medals.

2. World Championships in Athletics in 2023

Event dates: Budapest, Hungary, August 19–27, 2023

Events: Hassan is probably going to race in the 10,000 and 5,000 meters, and maybe even the 1,500 meters. She will use this event as a crucial stage to show the world's top athletes how competitive she is.

3. Diamond League Events Season: Every year, the Diamond League usually lasts from May through September.

Events: It is probable that Hassan will take part in a number of Diamond League meets, where she will be able to compete in her preferred distances and accumulate points for the Diamond League Final. She can assess her form and be ready for important competitions with these activities.

4. Championships of European Athletics
The European Athletics Championships in 2024 will take place in Rome, Italy.

Events: Hassan is anticipated to compete in the 1,500 and 5,000 meters with the goal of regaining her titles and solidifying her dominance in European athletics. Event Dates: August 7–12, 2024.

5. Possible Events for the First Marathon: As she continues to go toward longer distances, Hassan might think about competing in a significant marathon event, however this is not certain. Depending on her preparation and objectives, she might aim for races like the Berlin Marathon or the New York City Marathon.

6. Championships at the national level
Dutch National Championships: Hassan is eligible to participate in the Dutch National Championships, which offer her a chance to demonstrate her form at home and earn a spot on the national squad for competitions abroad.

7. Additional Regional Contests

International Road Races: In order to keep her competitive edge and gain experience in longer forms, Hassan may take part in regional or international road races, depending on her training regimen and recuperation requirements.

Sifan Hassan will have the chance to further her stellar career, defend her titles, and break new marks in her next challenges. Fans and competitors will be watching her closely as she gets ready for these big occasions, especially since she wants to leave her imprint at the World Athletics Championships and the Olympics in Paris. Her involvement in these events will inspire upcoming running generations and solidify her status in the sports world.

Potential for New Records

Sifan Hassan has a strong track record of pushing the limits of middle- and long-distance running, and she still can break records. Her prospective ability to break records is influenced by several factors:

Establishable Record-Breaking Capability

History of Record Success: Hassan has already clocked world records in the one-hour run (18.930 kilometers) and the mile (4:12.33). Her history of setting world records shows that she has a significant skill and a willingness to break records.

Recent Results: She has demonstrated her speed and endurance in significant competitions, which are essential for setting new records.

2. Adaptability Over Distances

Competing in Multiple races: Hassan can aim for multiple records because of her ability to compete successfully in both middle-distance (1,500m) and long-distance (5,000m, 10,000m) races. Because of her adaptability, she may target a variety of records based on her training priorities and race plan.

3. Conditioning and Strengthening

Constant Improvement: As an athlete, Hassan places a high priority on her strength and fitness because they can boost her output and increase her likelihood of setting new records. Her success can be attributed to her dedication to training and adapting her program.

Age and Experience: She will probably get better at her physical skills and racing tactics as she participates in more events, which could result in quicker times and new records.

4. A Competitive Setting

New Rivals and Competition: Hassan may be motivated to raise her game by the existence of formidable rivals. In high-stakes events like the Olympics and World Championships, competitors generally try to outperform one another in close races, which frequently results in record-breaking efforts.

Diamond League and Major Events: Because of the ideal racing conditions and competitive fields, competing in prestigious meets such as the Diamond League and major championships frequently results in faster times.

5. Concentrate on Your Future Prospects in the Marathon: Although Hassan hasn't made a name for herself in the longer distance, her move to it could have interesting outcomes. She can smash marathon records if she chooses to focus on this race because of her speed and endurance.

6. Resilience of Mind

Mental Fortitude: Hassan can function well under duress thanks to her mental toughness. Her ability to maintain concentration during crucial points of a race can result in records and personal bests.

7. Technological Advancements and Equipment Support: She may be able to shatter records and run faster thanks to advancements in technology and running shoes.

Coaching and Training Support: Hassan can maximize her performance and aim for record-breaking efforts if she has access to the best coaching and training tools, such as advanced analytics and recuperation procedures.

8. A goal-oriented strategy

Establishing Ambitious Goals: Hassan will strive to break new records because of her driven attitude and willingness to always push herself. Establishing quantifiable, precise objectives will help her stay focused on shattering current records.

Sifan Hassan has a great deal of potential to break records because of her remarkable track record, adaptability, and constant push for growth. Fans and observers will be closely observing her as she prepares for forthcoming events to see whether she can shatter previous records and establish new benchmarks in distance running. With her skills and the competitive landscape, Hassan's chances of hitting new professional highs are still very much alive.

Conclusion

Sifan Hassan's accomplishments in middle- and long-distance running serve as evidence of his exceptional physical prowess, tenacity, and adaptability. From her early years in Ethiopia to her ascent to the top of the global running rankings, Hassan has never stopped pushing boundaries, smashing records, taking home gold at the Olympics, and motivating a new generation of sportsmen.

She is a global sporting icon due to her extraordinary ability to balance several races, from the 1,500 meters to the marathon. She has gained respect and appreciation all around the world by continuously displaying the mental toughness and determination required for comebacks in the face of setbacks like injury.

In the future, Hassan has a ton of potential to do even more, such as setting additional records and performing exceptionally well in events like the 2024 Summer Olympics in Paris. Not only will she set the path for upcoming generations of runners with her athletic achievements, but she will also leave behind a legacy of excellence and tenacity that is sure to expand.

Sifan Hassan has already made a lasting impression on the distance-running community, and her journey is far from over.

Printed in Great Britain
by Amazon